Phil Collins

Biography

The Rhythm of a Remarkable Life

Ginger Helpenstill

Table of Content

Chapter 1: Not Drowning but Waving

We think mothers and fathers know everything. But in reality, they're making it up as they go. Every day, busking, winging it, and putting on a brave—sometimes deceptive—face. It's something I suspected as a youngster, but it wasn't verified until maturity, and then only with a little aid from the other side.

One dreary autumn evening in 1977, I went to see a medium. She lives in Victoria, central London, in a flat near the top of a tower block. It's not a gypsy caravan, but I suppose it means she's closer to the heavens. I don't have a special affinity for spirits—that will come much later, and it will be more of an addiction—but my wife, Andy, does. My mother, too, is no stranger to the Ouija board. My mother, nana, auntie, and so-called uncles Reg and Len spent many delightful late-fifties and early-sixties evenings conjuring the dearly departed from beyond the veil at our family home on London's suburban western outskirts. Better than the poor monochromatic choices flickering off the newfangled television set.

A misbehaving dog prompted my and Andy's visit to Madame Arcati, a high-rise. Ben, our gorgeous boxer, has a tendency of retrieving a pile of electric blankets from under our bed. We're saving these for our kids—Joely, five, and Simon, one—for when they stop wetting the bed and require some additional warmth. It has not occurred to me that the folded electric blankets promise more than just a warm bed—bent filaments can break and catch fire. Maybe Ben knows about this.

Andy concludes that Ben's nightly ritual contains a mystical aspect. He's probably not clairvoyant, but there's obviously something we humans don't know.

I'm now on tour with Genesis, having just released our record Wind & Wuthering and taking over singing responsibilities from Peter Gabriel. As a result, I am frequently an absent husband and father, and I feel perpetually behind in domestic and familial concerns. I have no objections to this unusual course of action.

So we'll go with a medium. Into crowded Victoria, up in the tower-block elevator, a ring on the doorstep, and light talk with the husband, who is watching Coronation Street. It couldn't be less spiritual. He turns away from the TV and gives me a nod: "She'll see you now…"
She's a normal-looking homemaker sat behind a tiny table. There is no trace of any otherworldly attributes. In fact, she appears completely normal and matter-of-fact. This absolutely surprises and disappoints me. My skepticism has taken on a new spin of bewilderment and grumpiness.
Andy's I Ching readings have shown that the spirits on my side of the family are the ones bothering the dogs, so I draw the short straw and enter the chamber of the otherworldly. Through gritted teeth, I inform the medium about Ben's nightly shenanigans. She nods sadly, closes her eyes, waits for a significant amount of time, and finally says, "It's your dad."
"Pardon?"
"Yes, it's your father, and he wants you to have a few items, including his watch, wallet, and the family cricket bat. You want me to invite his ghost to communicate through me? Then you heard his voice. However, sometimes the spirits refuse to go, which can be problematic.
I sputter, "No." When my father was living, our communication was not always smooth. Talking to him now, over five years after his death at Christmas 1972, through a middle-aged housewife in a depressingly dreary household setting in a tower block in the heart of London, would be strange.
"Well, he says to give your mum some flowers, and to tell her he's sorry."
Of course, as a very sensible twenty-six-year-old who prefers things to be straightforward and regimented—I am a drummer, after all—I should have dismissed this as nonsense con-artistry. But I agree that our dog's habit of dragging electric blankets from beneath our bed is not normal behavior. Furthermore, Madame Arcati has said things about my father that she could not have known, particularly about the

cricket bat. For as long as I can remember, the Collins clan's limited sporting equipment has included a cricket bat. Nobody outside the family would know about it. I would not say I'm convinced, but I'm curious. Andy and I leave the afterlife's anteroom and return to our normal lives. Back on solid ground, I inform her of the news. She responds with an understandable expression on both sides of the veil: "I told you so."

The next day, I call my mother and tell her about the previous evening's occurrences. She is unfazed by both the message and the medium.

"I bet he wants to give me flowers," she replies, partly joking and half harrumphing.

This is when she tells me everything. My father, Greville Philip Austin Collins, was not a loyal husband to my mother, June Winifred Collins (née Strange). He was recruited at the age of nineteen and worked for the London Assurance Company in the City of London for the rest of his life, just like his father. "Grev" had utilized his ordinary, bowler-hatted, nine-to-five suburban commuter existence to conceal a hidden relationship with an office girlfriend.

Now, nearly five years after Dad's death, while it is fantastic that my mother is confiding in me in this way, hearing these revelations makes me both angry and sad. My parents' marriage, I now know, did not dissolve so much as fizzle out, thanks in part to my father's, shall we say, distraction elsewhere. His infidelity was news to me.

Why wouldn't it be? I was a young boy at the time, and my parents appeared to be ecstatic. Life at home appeared to be normal and tranquil. Straightforward and simple. Mum and Dad were, in my opinion, happily in love throughout their long marriage.

But I'm the baby of the family, about seven years younger than my sister Carole and nine years younger than my brother Clive. Certain mature aspects of home life would have gone right over my head. Now, as I study the facts before me this evening in 1977, I believe I can detect an undercurrent of dissatisfaction in the house, of which I was absolutely unaware at the time. However, perhaps I felt it in my water: I was a chronic bed-wetter till an embarrassingly elderly age.

I am disappointed to having been married three times. I'm even more dissatisfied because I've been divorced three times. I'm much less disturbed that this led in settlements with my ex-wives totaling £42 million. I'm not bothered that the figures were publicly reported and are well recognized. Nothing is truly private in today's world. The internet has ensured that. Furthermore, while three divorces may appear to indicate a careless attitude toward the entire concept of marriage, this could not be further from the truth. I'm a romantic who believes, and hopes, that marriage is something to love and preserve.

I have tried to be honest with all of my children about my personal history. It involves them. It impacts them. Every day, they face the consequences of my acts, inactions, and emotions. I strive to be as honest and upfront as possible. I'll do the same throughout this novel, even when things don't go so well. As a drummer, I am used to giving it some stick. I've got to get used to take some stick, too. On January 30, 1951, I was born in Putney Maternity Hospital, southwest London, as June and Grev Collins' belated—and, by all accounts, unexpected—third child. Mum apparently entered West Middlesex Hospital to have me, but they were not very pleasant to her, so she crossed her legs, left, and went to Putney.

I was the first "London" child, as Carole and Clive were born at Weston-super-Mare after London Assurance relocated the entire family there prior to the Blitz. Carole was not too delighted with my birth. She'd wanted a girl. Clive, on the other hand, was overjoyed— he finally had a small brother to play football with, wrestle with, and, when that got dull, pin down and torture with his stinking socks.

My arrival made Mum and Dad, who were thirty-seven and forty-five years old at the time, old parents. This did not concern my mother in the slightest. She was a generous and caring woman her entire life, never saying anything negative about anyone until her death on her ninety-eighth birthday in 2011. However, she reportedly called a

London police officer a "dickhead" when he chastised her for driving in a bus lane.

According to family history, two of Dad's relatives were detained by the Japanese in Singapore's renowned Changi Prison. They placed a high value on themselves—they were combat heroes who had survived the harrowing Far East conflict. Another cousin appears to have been the first to introduce laundromats to England. Dad's family saw each of them as "somebody." In other words, toffs. H. G. Wells was believed to be a frequent caller at the Collins home.

There's little evidence that Grev Collins ever adapted to the twentieth century. When North Sea gas became available and all boilers in the United Kingdom were converted, Dad attempted to bribe the Gas Board to exclude us from the conversions. Dad believed that somewhere there was a gasholder that would produce fuel only for the Collins family.

Dad enjoyed cleaning the dishes, and he insisted on doing it on Sundays after the family lunch. He loved doing this alone because it allowed him to avoid mingling at the table. All would be well until a crash erupted from the kitchen. All conversation would end, and Mum would go to the French windows and close the curtains. Dad could be heard swearing loudly shortly after the accident, followed by the sound of crockery being swept into a pan. The back door would be yanked open and the crockery strewn noisily into the garden, where Dad would kick it around outside the window, accompanied by more loud swearing.

Dad was not ignorant of home improvement, but he had no genuine interest in it. He believed that if things worked well, all was well. This was especially relevant to electricity. In the early 1950s, the plugs were brown Bakelite, and the wires were covered with a woven ribbon. They were fairly unreliable, and in the back room, where the radio was stored, the main socket on the skirting board frequently fed five or six other plugs. Electricians would call it a "Christmas tree." Ours was always fizzing, which is not a sound you want to hear when it comes to residential electricity, and as the eldest, Clive was always chosen to insert another plug into the already overloaded socket. Carole and I would watch with naughty fascination as he invariably felt a tiny shock run up his arm like a violent tickle.

"That suggests there is power there. Dad would say, "No problem with that," before sitting down with his pipe to listen to the radio or watch TV, oblivious to poor Clive and his smoking arm.

Prior to my arrival, the family did not own a car because Dad did not pass his driving exam until 1952, one year after I was born. This was only his seventh attempt. If the automobile didn't "behave" itself, Dad would swear at it, convinced that the malfunctioning motor was part of a plot against him. The iconic scene from Fawlty Towers, with John Cleese's Basil Fawlty flogging his traitorous Austin 1100 Countryman, accurately depicts our family life.

Dad was so stuck in the past that when decimalization was implemented in 1971, he declared that it would be the last of him. The nation's new coinage represented a new threat. Taking the long perspective, I have no reason to doubt that the demise of the shilling contributed to his death from worry.

Mum was another seasoned Londoner. She grew raised on Fulham's North End Road as one of three seamstress sisters. Her brother, Charles, was a Spitfire pilot who was shot down and killed during the war. Gladys, one of her sisters, resided in Australia, and we traded audio CDs every Christmas. She died before I could meet her. Auntie Florrie, Mum's other sister, was delightful, and as a child, I'd pay her a weekly visit at her flat in Dolphin Square, Pimlico. My maternal grandmother, Nana to me, was a darling and another significant female influence on my early self.

By the time I arrived, just over sixteen years later, the Collins family had relocated to Whitton in Richmond-upon-Thames. Then followed a big, three-story Edwardian mansion at 34 St. Leonards Road in East Sheen, another southwest London neighborhood.

Because Mum worked full-time at the toyshop, Nana cared after me while Clive and Carole were at school. Nana adored me, and we developed a wonderful close friendship. She'd wheel me around Upper

Richmond Road in our pram, stopping at the baker's to purchase me a penny bun. The fact that I remember this daily treat so vividly demonstrates my close relationship with my grandmother.

As is customary, the house you live in as a child appears to be large. Visiting it years later can be shocking. How did everyone fit in there? Mum and Dad presumably have the master bedroom, with Carole in a modest room next door. Clive and I are on bunk beds in the back of the house. Our room is so dim that we have to step outside to alter our minds. By the time I'm a teen, there's barely enough room beneath my bed to hide the collection of girlie magazines that has somehow ended up in my possession. We shared those apartments throughout my childhood until 1964, when Clive, then twenty-two, left home.

Being born in the early 1950s means growing up in a London that is still healing from Hitler's hammering. However, I have no memories of bomb sites or any other type of devastation in our neighborhood.

The only time I recall witnessing anything resembling the aftermath of a bombing was when the family went into the city for Dad's office events. London Assurance staged performances with their dramatic society, and the family made the lengthy journey from Hounslow, via Cripplegate, to London's financial center. My memories of such travels include visions of flattened wasteland around the ancient London Wall, reminiscent of scenes from the 1947 Ealing comedy Hue and Cry, complete with street urchins playing among the wreckage.

In fact, the London of my childhood was similar to that of those Ealing comedies or of my comedy hero, Tony Hancock, who lived at the fake London suburban address of 23 Railway Cuttings, East Cheam. There is little traffic to speak of, even in central London, and certainly no delays or parking issues—Reg and Len's home-movie footage of the Great West Road shows how few cars pass by. Droves of bowler-hatted men plodding across Waterloo Bridge. Football throng, flat-capped to a man. Holidays at the seaside—in our family's case, Bognor Regis or Selsey Bill in West Sussex—with the guys getting into the beachside spirit by possibly removing their shirts and ties.

How do I feel about growing up at the end of the line? Everything is a walk, followed by a bus, another short walk, and finally a train. Everything is an effort. So you have your own pleasure. Unfortunately, some children's enjoyment does not extend to mine.

At Nelson Infants School, I appear to be routinely bullied by Kenny Broder, a student at St. Edmund's Primary, which is conveniently located right across the street. He is only ten years old, like me, but he has a boxer's look, with high cheekbones and a nose that has seen some action. I'm afraid Broder will emerge from his school gates at the same moment I leave mine. He'll eyeball me the entire way home, subtly threatening violence. I feel like I'm constantly being picked on—and for no apparent reason. Is there a target on my forehead or a "kick me" sign on the back of my shorts?

Even my first encounter with the opposite sex is distorted by the lens of schoolboy aggression. I take Linda, my first girlfriend, to a funfair on Hounslow Heath, my pockets bursting with the hard-earned coins that will get us through the helter-skelter of love and/or the dodgems, whichever has the shortest line. No sooner had we arrived than a shiver ran up my neck. "Oh God," according to me, "there's Broder and his gang."

Still, at the age of twelve, I manage to lose my fighting virginity at the park next to my mother's toyshop. We usually assemble here, beside a large horse trough from years past and a slip road where the 657 trolley buses turn around. Because this is the end of the line.

So, the park is our territory. I don't belong to a legitimate gang; we're simply a bunch of young wannabe toughs out to protect our area. Especially if there are some bigger local lads there to provide backup. We both believe we came to a respectful close. But then the older lads arrive and insist on securing our advantage. They demanded I tell them where the infiltrators were. Big Fat Dave—not generally addressed in this manner, especially by me—sets out to "sort him out." He ignores my shouts of "Stop, we agreed it was a draw!". I feel bad because, from a distance, I see Big Fat Dave hopping up and down on my adversary's bike, which is parked opposite the sweet shop. Oh well, at least they won't be bothering with Hounslow for a bit.

The Duke of Wellington, the local bar, quickly becomes a favorite hangout, and I befriend the landlord's son. Charles Salmon is a few years younger than me, but we quickly became friends. During our adolescence, we develop shared bad habits, such as stealing alcoholic beverages from the pub's on-site off-license and pilfering cigarettes by the fistful when Charles' older sister Teddy is behind the counter. We go to his garden shed and smoke until we become sick. I smoke anything, including cigars, cigarillos, and French cigarettes. By the time I'm 15, I'm smoking a pipe like my father.

I also made acquainted with local boys Arthur Wild and his younger brother Jack. Jack and I's lives will eventually intersect: as young actors, we share a West End stage, with him playing Charley Bates, best friend to my Artful Dodger, in the inaugural production of Oliver! the musical. He will, however, outperform me by portraying The Dodger in Carol Reed's Oscar-winning 1968 film.

Football is an important part of my life, as it is for any young boy. In the early 1960s, I was a die-hard Tottenham Hotspur supporter who idolized goal-scoring dynamo Jimmy Greaves. My fondness for the team is so strong that I can still name them. But Spurs are a north London team, and north London could as well be Mars. I would never dare to step so far outside of my comfort zone.

Grev and June Collins are both boat enthusiasts and help administer the newly established Converted Cruiser Club. They are members of a large, river-loving social group that includes Reg and Len Tungay, the previously mentioned uncles. The brothers have their yacht, Sadie. She's another war veteran, a member of the Dunkirk flotilla, and her craft is large enough for us to sleep on, which I do on many wonderful occasions.

An annual event is held at Platt's Ait near Hampton, where club members spend the weekend with their beloved boats, competing in rowing races, tug-of-wars, and knot-tying competitions. I've been handling a rope and rowing a dinghy since I was very little, and I've never been afraid of water. For a tiny chap like me, this is heady stuff that promotes a fantastic sense of community. In today's environment, that may sound a little uninteresting, but not in my youth. I even consider it a privilege to attend Nelson Infants. As a side note to the ocean and its impact on our family, my father never learned to swim. His father ingrained in him the phobia of ever being more than waist-deep in water. Anything more and he'd drown. He believed him. And here is the man who attempted to flee and join the merchant marine.

In some manner, the Thames has played an important role in my early life. I've spent most weekends rowing between bridges since I was a child. The Converted Cruiser Club does not yet have its own clubhouse, so we meet and socialize at Dick Waite's Boatyard on the riverbank at St. Margarets, where Dad moors his little motorboat, Teuke. Pete Townshend eventually buys the property and turns it into his Meher Baba Oceanic recording studio. I made him a replica of an old photograph of me in my mother's arms taken on the exact same area. Pete, ever the gentleman, wrote me a lovely, tear-stained letter of thanks. The photograph hung in the studio for several years.

By the late 1950s, the club is renting a plot on Eel Pie Island for a penny per year. I spent a significant amount of my early years helping to build the permanent clubhouse and then participating in the shows and pantomimes produced by the members. I can legitimately claim to have performed at this historic theater in the heart of the Thames—the epicenter of the British blues revolution in the 1960s—long before The Rolling Stones, Rod Stewart, and The Who.

Aside from that, I'm still fooling around on the river. However, these frequent boat club revues eventually provide me with the opportunity to play drums in public for the first time. There is footage of a ten-year-old me performing with the Derek Altman All-Stars, led by the squeezebox maestro. Carole and Clive are also performing comic routines. Mum also does her part, singing "Who's Sorry Now?" with passion.

I'm overcome with melancholy when I think of the situation. There were so many questions I could have asked my father if I'd known I'd just be twenty-one when he passed. Simply said, there wasn't much closeness or communication between us. Maybe I blocked out the recollections. Maybe they do not exist.

I recall vividly bedwetting and sleeping with a rubber sheet under a cotton sheet. If I "have an accident," the rubber sheet just keeps the dampness from spreading, causing me to sleep in a little pool of trapped wee. What would you do in this scenario? You go to sleep with your mother and father, then pee their bed. This must really endear me to my father. We don't have a shower in our small semi-detached house, and early-morning baths are uncommon, so I'm afraid Dad will go to work with a faint odor of pee for the next few years.

Regardless of how much he loves the river, Dad can't help but revert to his occasionally callous behavior. I have cinematic proof. Reg Tungay's home movie captures me and Dad at the water's edge on Eel Pie Island. I'm about six. There is a fifteen-foot plunge below me into the Thames.

I'm not saying he didn't care, but I believe he occasionally didn't think. Perhaps he was distracted by something else as he left me hanging on the edge of the Thames. He was making it up every day.

That is something I would do in adulthood too. Partly in a positive, creative way—I'm a songwriter and performer, and making stuff up is an essential part of the work. But also, I admit, in a bad sense. As I traversed the world for nearly four decades, both with Genesis and as a solo artist, I was continually bolstering a fiction: that I could have a stable family life while also pursuing a musical career.

We mothers and fathers don't know everything. Far from it.

Chapter 2: Traveling to the Beat of a Different Drum

The Tungay boys, frequent visitors to 453 Hanworth Road, particularly for Sunday lunch—a weekly opportunity for Mum to assiduously boil all the greens until they're grays—notice my fondness for percussive and rhythmic elements. Perhaps they are less aware of my father's point of view on the matter.

When I'm five years old, Reg and Len put together a homemade setup for me. Two pieces of wood are fastened into a crosspiece. Each end has a drilled hole through which a pole can be put. The four poles are topped with two biscuit tins, a triangle, and a cheap plastic tambourine. It collapses and fits nicely into a brown suitcase.

Calling this a drum "kit" is pushing it. It's more Heath Robinson than Buddy Rich. But I'm in heaven, and this crash-bang-wallop gear will be both my musical tools and closest buddy for the next few noisy years.

As I reach adolescence, my commitment grows stronger. Piece by piece, I put together a nice kit. The snare drum is followed by a cymbal, then by a bass drum purchased from the guy across the street. This will tide me over till I am twelve. Now that I'm approaching my adolescence, Mum has agreed to split the cost of a decent kit with me. It is 1963, and the 1960s are in full swing. The Beatles have arrived, and the future can begin. Their debut single, "Love Me Do," was released the previous October, and Beatlemania has already firmly gripped my attention. I make the ultimate sacrifice: I'm going to sell my brother's toy train set to cover my part of the deal I made with Mum. It does not occur to me that I should have sought his consent.

Mum and I head to Albert's Music Shop in Twickenham, where we spend £50 on a four-piece Stratford outfit in white pearl. I'm sitting at that kit in the portrait of myself as a thirteen-year-old on the cover of my 2010 album, Going Back.

I believe my drumming abilities are improving, thanks in part to the fact that I practice whenever feasible. My neighbors at 451 and 455

Hanworth Road would probably corroborate that I put in my 10,000 hours before I was even a teenager. When I'm at home, I drum almost exclusively, as the teachers who graded my coursework at Nelson Infants and then Chiswick County Grammar will most likely attest. Around this time, I also experience a terrible but mercifully brief bout of childhood modeling. I star in advertising and knitting patterns alongside half a dozen other adolescent boys, all of whom are staring intently into the middle distance. I have a flicky blond fringe and a cherubic smile, and I look great in pajamas and woolen sweaters.

Still reeling from my Shakespearean Humpty Dumpty and thrilled by my proto-Zoolander modeling brilliance, my excited mother coerces me into spending Saturday mornings taking elocution lessons in a dour basement on Jocelyn Road in Richmond, taught by a lady named Hilda Rowland. There's linoleum on the floor, ballerina mirrors on the wall, and a faint odor of feminine hormones in the air. Mrs. Rowland has a wonderful acquaintance named Barbara Speake, who established her dancing school in Acton in 1945. My mother develops friends with Miss Speake. Mum, who has ceased managing the toyshop, joins her in founding the school's theatrical agency from our house. June Collins provides all-singing, all-dancing children to London's West End and the burgeoning commercial television and film industries.

Children are constantly in demand during the early days of television advertising. The Milky Bar Kid is the best role to land. Casting this and many other ads confronts my mother with a daily dilemma as she determines which child she represents would best fit the role. She really immerses herself in this, which is how, in 1964, she learns about Oliver auditions! The successful Lionel Bart musical adaption of Charles Dickens' Oliver Twist is presently in its fourth year of a ten-year run. I'm going for the role of The Artful Dodger, which future Monkee Davy Jones has previously portrayed and will play again in the Broadway transfer.

After numerous auditions and recalls, much to the astonishment and joy of my thirteen-year-old self, I was cast in the role. I am cock-a-hoop. Dodger, the street-smart, wisecracking kid, is my favorite character on the program. Oliver, that smirking goody two shoes? There's no chance.

I set an appointment with my headmaster at Chiswick County Grammar to tell him the good news. Mr. Hands scares the entire student body. He is a strict old-school educator who always enters assembly with his robe flowing like bat wings, mortar board firmly placed on his head, cheeks ruddy and ready for a day of rigorous study. The restrictions restricting under-fifteens working in the West End at the time were stringent. The longest you can perform anyplace is nine months. This consists of three three-month contracts, with each child receiving three weeks off. Mr. Hands cannot tolerate such term-time laxity. Reg and Len would subsequently inform me that he was very interested in and proud of my achievements. This is surprising given that he has always appeared to be completely uninterested in entertainment. The jury is still out on whether Mr. Hands was more of a Genesis or Phil Collins man.

In many ways, this will be a win-win for me. For one thing, I can act as much as I want. For another, at the Barbara Speake Stage School, girls outweigh boys by a significant amount. I'm in the newly established "student class" with one other boy, Philip Gadd, and a dozen girls.

In fact, it's a win-win situation. My official education comes to an end at this time, as my focus is solely on improving performance, auditioning, and landing parts. This is nirvana for me, a regular adolescent lad. It's only later that I'll wish I had more standard education and less ballet. However, I would have like to study tap dance. It's something all great early hitters, including Buddy Rich, knew how to do. Similarly, famous dancers like Fred Astaire were also excellent drummers. The two skills are close rhythmic cousins, and I wish I had shown more interest. Who wouldn't have enjoyed a few taps at Live Aid?

I am thirteen years old when I join in stage school. My adolescence begins with a boom, in every way. I am a popular drummer at school. My performing colleagues are envious of my role in a major West End production. And I am one of only two lads in a class filled with gregarious, artistically inclined girls.

I hesitate to say that I squired my way through the entire student body over my four years at acting school, but I believe there were only one or two girls who avoided my notice. I've never been this cool. I'll never be this cool again.

According to history, I first had sex when I was fourteen. I say "suggests" because it happened so rapidly that it may not be considered part of the intercourse. However, as a horny kid in a close-knit suburban area, your choices are restricted. By the time you're in a circumstance where it could happen, you'll be in danger and out of the starting gate. So Cheryl—who, like me, is fourteen and a wannabe Mod—and I get dirty in an allotment. I didn't intend to be outside in the mud, surrounded by small plots of potatoes and carrots, but I didn't have much choice.

My first year of adolescence was significant. In early 1964, my acting agent—my mother—tells me to go to the Scala Theatre on Charlotte Street in central London. As I go in on the Piccadilly Line that afternoon, I have no idea what the work involves. I believe that's part of the strategy, because none of the throngs of teenagers gathered inside the theater appear to understand what's going on. If you want a true audience response, gather a group of youngsters in front of a stage that is empty save for some musical instruments, and don't tell them who is going to appear.

Having said that, I have some insider information: Ringo Starr's Ludwig drum equipment is easily identifiable anyplace. But I would not have imagined The Beatles were creating a film.

There was a sudden ruckus in the wings. As if by magic, Ringo, John Lennon, Paul McCartney, and George Harrison appear on stage, dressed in beautiful gray mohair suits with black collars. The Scala Theatre erupted.

This is a performance scene in A Hard Day's Night, which will serve as the film's finale. When they film us youngsters in the audience, there are stand-ins onstage. But when John, Paul, George, and Ringo play, they're just about 30 feet away from me. As a paid-up member of The Beatles fan club, I can't believe my luck. Not only am I in the spotlight at an intimate performance (of sorts), but I am also being immortalized on celluloid alongside my earliest musical heroes.

If only. Master Philip Collins is conspicuously absent from the picture, which was released in cinemas that summer. That day, my performance is cut short. Wasn't I screaming enough?

Let's fast forward to the early 1990s. The film's producer, Walter Shenson, pays me a visit at Genesis' recording studio, The Farm, in Surrey. On the 30th anniversary of A Hard Day's Night, I was asked to record the narration for a DVD documentary on the film's production process. He sends me the outtakes for "my" scenes.

This was "Tell Me Why," "She Loves You," and "All My Loving," the songs that were sparking my rapidly developing musical synapses. This, I realized, was my future, and I wanted to embrace it. Forget bloody acting. That may have been why I was there in the first place, but in the grand scheme of things, I was completely indifferent.

The show times for Oliver! require me to travel to the West End straight from stage school every day. Still, I normally arrive in Soho about 4 p.m., with plenty of time to kill. I frequently pop into one of the small cinemas spread across downtown London that show cartoons on an hourly rotation. I believe these are intended for commuters having a few minutes before the next train. Unbeknownst to me, they have another purpose. In Britain, where homosexuality remains illegal, men utilize them as discreet(ish) pick-up spots. One time, a guy approached me during a Loony Tunes cartoon and tentatively placed a hand on my boyish knee. I growl, "Fuck off," and he flees quicker than the Road Runner.

Over the next few months, I became accustomed to this dark side of the West End, and these overtures became almost tediously ritualistic. My afternoons and nights form a joyful routine: train from Hounslow, film, a stroll through Soho coffee bars and record shops, and a short burger at Wimpy. Then I proceed to the New Theatre's stage door on St. Martin's Lane, near Trafalgar Square.

Furthermore, this is a significant contribution. The Artful Dodger's entry marks the beginning of the show. This tale of Victorian workhouses and grinding poverty is mostly doom and despair until the chirpy, light-fingered urchin appears and sings "Consider Yourself." The Dickensian East End of Lionel Bart's picaresque, exuberant imagination explodes into spectacular life. Consider that the Dodger and his band also perform fantastic, now-classic tunes like "I'd Do Anything" and "Be Back Soon". They're my first lead vocals, and I enjoy performing them eight nights a week (including matinees on Wednesdays and Saturdays).

There are also fringe benefits. While I'm onstage at the New Theatre, my girlfriend Lavinia is performing in The Prime of Miss Jean Brodie at Wyndham's Theatre, just yards away. Their stage door backs up to our. Our intervals don't always coincide, but there's typically enough time to sneak out and meet the love of your adolescent life for a short snog and cuddle before the concert starts.

While watching Oliver!, I celebrate my fourteenth birthday, and change is in the air. One night, I'm in the middle of "Consider Yourself," belting it out with the appropriate joyful, cheeky fervor. Then, from the back of my usually golden throat, a squawk and a croak, and my singing voice abruptly stops. I struggle on valiantly, but at the intermission, I hurry to the stage manager. I don't comprehend what happened to my voice. I don't have a cold, I've never had any difficulty singing before, not even on a bad night, and it can't be the fags. I've been a pro-smoker for several years thanks to petty larceny from the off-license at Charles Salmon's father's tavern.

The stage manager, an experienced West End wrangler of many a kid actor, tells me the truth: my voice is failing.

Forget any encouraging signs that I'm growing into a man, my child. Right now, in the wings, crouched behind the safety curtain, I am distraught. I understand what this means.

I get through the second part, but my voice is shot. The entire auditorium is aware of it. Beyond the stage lights, I can hear a shuffle in the stall. It is an awful feeling. I despise disappointing an audience, a neurotic fear that I will carry with me forever. I can count on one hand the amount of gigs I canceled with Genesis or on my own tours. Over the course of my career, I will do whatever it takes to keep the show running, even if it means dealing with shady doctors, receiving questionable injections, suffering catastrophic hearing, and sustaining injuries that will necessitate massive, invasive, flesh-ripping, bone-bolting surgery.

However, that marks the end of my time as The Artful Dodger, the best part for a kid in London. With emotionless efficiency, I'm instantly removed from the play, cast out of the West End, and returned to the end of the line.

For a hormonal young kid enamored with everything an increasingly swinging mid-sixties London has to offer, Oliver! has been a trip both on and offstage. During my seven months of joyfully indentured West End service, I get to know the house musicians of the New Theatre. The bandleader is a drummer, and fortunately, he and I ride the same train home. We communicate. So I converse with him, asking for details about a musician's life, and he patiently responds. I quickly realize that being a jobbing player in show bands, orchestra pits, and clubs is an excellent career path. I'll take that.

At this moment, I am a completely self-taught musician. However, I recognize that if I want to become a professional, I must improve my performance.

I begin piano lessons with my Great-Auntie Daisy at her musty Edwardian home on Netheravon Road, Chiswick. She's charming, patient, and helpful, and it comes naturally to me, which surprises both of us. When I hear something, I never have to look at the page again. I have what they call "big ears," which are fantastic for memorizing songs but less so for learning to read music. This irritates Auntie Daisy, but she does not hold it against me. When she died, I inherited her 1820 straight-strung Collard & Collard. I plan to use the piano to record the entirety of my first solo album, Face Value.

Nine years after receiving my first kit from Uncle Reg and Uncle Len, I finally decide to start drum lessons. When I start attending Barbara

Speake's, my route to school from Acton Town station up Churchfield Road passes a drum shop operated by Maurice Plaquet. This location is a paradise for players from all around London, and Maurice is a well-known session drummer who I am eager to join. He's too big a fish to teach me, so I approach one of his lieutenants, Lloyd Ryan, who teaches from Maurice's basement.

At the end of the 1960s, during another brief West End acting run (back in Oliver!, but in a more mature character this time, that of cowardly bully Noah Claypole), I took some lessons from a lovely man named Frank King. He teaches at Chas E. Foote's, a classic drummer's shop located directly across from the stage door of my then-day job at the Piccadilly Theatre. That's the extent of my official musical instruction. I've taken maybe thirty drum lessons in my life.

Fashion evolves in tandem with musical trends. It's 1966, and I'm shopping at I Was Lord Kitchener's Valet on Foubert's Place, just off Carnaby Street, which is currently the most popular boutique. I'm looking for the military clothing that major figures on the scene are wearing, particularly two musicians in a new band with whom I've grown infatuated. Eric Clapton and Ginger Baker are the cool-as-they-come lead guitarist and mad-as-a-hatter drummer in Cream, which history will remember as rock's first supergroup.

My introduction to Cream occurs, ironically, in good old Hounslow. One night in 1966, I'm waiting for the last bus at Hounslow bus station when I hear a raucous blues band pounding through the walls of The Attic, a local bar. I'm fifteen, and I hear Cream playing songs from their debut album, Fresh Cream, which will be published at the end of the year. I never imagined that I would eventually become a great buddy, sideman, producer, and party companion to their already explosive guitarist.

Yes, 1966 is the year England won the World Cup. But it's a golden year for me for another reason: I create my first band with some other Barbara Speake students. The Real Thing consists of me on drums, Philip Gadd on guitar, his brother Martin on bass, and Peter Newton on lead vocals. Lavinia and Andy, two of the most important women in my life, provide supporting vocals.

We are drama school kids who are accustomed to slacking off in class and listening to the latest platters by The Beatles and The Byrds while studying, and we go for it with gusto. We don't travel or gig much farther than Acton, though. Even East Acton is out of bounds. It's lethal for us theater kids because it's the location of Faraday School, which is packed with hard nuts who enjoy nothing more than duffing up a boy who wears tights. Poor black Peter lives near East Acton Station, which is in a danger zone. His skin color suggests he is beaten with greater frequency and enjoyment.

Undaunted (mainly), The Real Thing absorbs soul and Motown music and performs cover versions of everything they can discover. Essentially, we are ripping from The Action's setlist. They are a group of sharp-dressed Mods from Kentish Town, northwest London, whose slinky 1965 debut song, "Land of a Thousand Dances," was produced by George Martin. Peter and I consider ourselves their biggest fans. I'm still a fan in 1969, when they rename themselves Mighty Baby. In 2000, Mod guru Rob Bailey sends me the phone number of The Action's Roger Powell, who is arguably my biggest drumming influence. I call him and we become best friends. Because of our acquaintance, I had the opportunity to join the reunited Action for a gig at the 100 Club on Oxford Street in London. Playing beside my hero Roger, I finally get to meet the complete band 40 years after pursuing them at the Marquee. I'm not exaggerating when I tell The Guardian that it felt like I was playing with The Beatles.

We strive to mimic The Action in every manner. Roger has a nice blue nylon jacket. As a fanboy and clotheshorse, I manage to find one similar to it after scouring Carnaby Street's prominent Mod retailers. After a few weeks of use, my mother washes it. It somehow gets shrunk and shredded. It is ruined. For a young Mod, this is a knife to the heart.

The Marquee, in its several iterations on Wardour Street, currently lacks a proper bar. You can only buy Coca-Cola from a little stall in the back. The priority is gig space, which can accommodate up to 1,200 people. This is definitely beyond fire rules. But no one cares about such safety concerns, just as they do not care about automobile seat belts, cancer-causing cigarettes, or 100,000 men and boys crammed into football terraces with no seating or crushing barriers. Simpler times. If you managed to survive them.

The Marquee is now installing a decent bar, which reduces capacity by roughly half yet does not diminish excitement. These are the days when someone will join a band in the day and then play with them at night. Jeff Beck joins The Yardbirds one afternoon, and Jimmy Page another. I'm in the audience for their two debuts.

I'm a fan of the Yardbirds, and when they reformed as The New Yardbirds, I became a fan of their drummer, John Bonham. With Roger from The Action, he is my drumming hero. I went to see Tim Rose—I adore the American singer-songwriter, and I especially enjoy his interpretation of Bonnie Dobson's "Morning Dew"—because Bonham is his hired drummer for the tour. My oldest friend, Ronnie Caryl, and I still speak about that Marquee performance—"My God, what was he doing with his foot?" Bonham was fantastic.

In my mid-teens in mid-sixties London, Santa Claus's gift to the three-year-old me is the gift that keeps on giving. The first child's drum set me on a path that led me to the core of a revolution. The drums will continue to force me forward, upward, and occasionally even sideways. But right now, they've triggered something that's causing me to become increasingly agitated.

At this point, I am still a kid. A schoolboy. And a schoolboy from the far west, in the increasingly claustrophobic sticks. This starts to bother me when it interferes with my ability to attend gigs. The Marquee's nighttime performance schedule is often as follows: support band, headliner, support band, headliner again. I normally see the first three, but I have to leave before the third headliner's set to get the train home by 10:30 p.m., which is my curfew. Then, on January 24, 1967, Jimi Hendrix makes his debut at the Marquee. This was the first of the tyro American guitarist's four epic gigs there, and it will go down in rock history as one of the defining rock shows of the 1960s. He was one among the first entertainers to perform one big set rather than two.

Typically, I am the first to arrive and secure a front-row seat. However, in exasperation, I am forced to leave before Hendrix performs. The final train to the end of the line is calling.

The faster I get out of there, the better.

Chapter 3: "Drummer Seeks Band; Has Own Sticks"

I had to get out of this place. But how? It won't be through London Assurance, despite my father's valiant efforts to encourage me to carry on the family legacy. I am a time-serving child of the 1960s, and the nine-to-five is definitely not for me, papa.

So, how can I escape, and by what means? Music is my passion, and London is the global hub of the entire industry. Stuck at the end of the Piccadilly Line, my drum skills growing with each session, it feels like I'm so close but so far. I need an exit strategy, and ideally someone to accompany me. Fortunately, I know just the person.

In early 1966, at the age of fifteen, I learn of a boy who appears to be as talented on the guitar as I am on the drums. He's from Hanworth, just down the road from Hounslow, and he attends the Corona Academy, a rival performing arts school. The inter-drama-school rumor mill has made us all aware of one another, and each of us is deemed "cool" by the cliques at our separate song'n'dance alma maters.

Actually, if I may say so, we're getting along really well. I have a tape of Ronnie and me playing for hours on end, and it still sounds very impressive. Despite the fact that there are only two of us, we are both talented musicians, and the combination is full and bluesy.

We eventually recruit a bassist, Anthony Holmes, who is a friend of a friend. But it quickly becomes apparent that, despite owning a bass, he cannot play it. This does not deter Anthony, however. He just plays extremely quietly, so it's difficult to say whether he can or cannot. With our concerts confined to my parents' front room, this isn't a big deal, nor is our lack of a band name. We soon learned practically the complete track listing for Fresh Cream. We also discovered John Mayall and an outstanding library of classic blues songs. If we're not exactly a supergroup, we're definitely a delectable trio.

Then Donegan suggests that he could be looking for a drummer, and for a brief moment, I picture a bright future ahead of me, contributing to the continuation of a musical revolution that, to be honest, has passed its skiffle-by date. Unfortunately, I believe Donegan has no intention of recruiting Carole Collins' fifteen-year-old brother, if only because I am too young for the rigors of his hectic gigging schedule. He does, however, believe I'm talented enough to offer to look for a band that might recruit me. Despite his zeal, nothing shows itself.

Shortly after, Anthony hangs up his bass for good, but Ronnie and I persevere. We are best friends until the end of our lives. Our friendship is honest to the point of combustibility. We've had plenty of terrible arguments, generally after a few beers. Ronnie will be missing a tooth by the late 1960s, thanks to my fist. It is not something I am proud of, and I will never do it to anyone again.

Ronnie and I will embark on numerous adventures as musical companions and bandmates over the next fifty years. At one end of the timeline, we will both try for Genesis. Later on, while I'm recording my sixth solo album, 1996's Dance into the Light, I realize I'll need a second guitarist to complement the long-serving Daryl Stuermer. I invite my oldest friend to attend rehearsals in Switzerland.

Within a few weeks, Ronnie is fully integrated, and harmony prevails, as I expected. I told my oldest friend, "As long as I'm working, you're working." When I need a guitarist, he is my first choice. Everything is the same as it has always been. Such are the soul-solid links formed in the fire of first musical loves. Those friendships will carry me through my sixties musical finishing school, from bedroom practice sessions to pubs, clubs, holiday-camp gigs, and beyond.

By 1967, The Real Thing were less of a certainty. The exuberant enthusiasm we had for our first school combo has evolved into the serious business of being professional dancers or actors, albeit less so for me than for my former bandmates. But, as a cocky sixteen-year-old, I'm confident a clear route will open up ahead of me. To be honest, I'm not certain that this relatively new pop group "thing" will continue that long. If it does, it will almost definitely not involve me. But I'll ride it till it burns out, after which I'll do some recording sessions for others. After a good run of studio work, I'll transition into a show band/big band/jazz setting. I'm already listening to Buddy Rich, Count Basie, and John Coltrane, so this feels like a natural continuation. I'll then spend the rest of my life playing in the orchestra pit for one of London's finest theatre plays. The players I encountered while filming Oliver! all appeared to be in good spirits.

Again, this appears to be a logical line of action. However, it will require learning to read music. I'll get to it sometime soon.

With some experience under my belt and now as a senior student at Barbara Speake's, I'm getting a lot of acting offers. Most of them I decline, much to my mother's displeasure. But I decide to accept a cinema job provided by the Children's Film Foundation, which provides healthy films for Saturday morning movie groups. By the mid-sixties, these had grown in prominence, not least because they provided a safe location for parents to leave their children while shopping. So what if the small film, Calamity the Cow, lacks wonderful psychedelia? It implies that youngsters from all over the country will see me on the big screen. It also means I'll be able to spend more money on records, concert tickets, and cod-military gear. Plus, I have the biggest part—aside from the cow, of course.

The filming takes place in Guildford, which, coincidentally, will become my hometown some years later, when Eric Clapton and I will be country neighbors. But in 1967, Guildford represented a place that appears to be miles away from Hounslow, and it is the setting for a pig farm so vile that I can still smell it today.

The warm Summer of Love It is clear that accepting the lead role in this film was a bad decision on my behalf. Because this is a CFF production intended for Saturday morning pleasure, we must keep things lighthearted. Very young. Enid Blyton is young. The plot can be summarized as follows: boy finds cow, loses cow, then finds cow. I should be tuning in, turning on, and then dropping out. Instead, I'm getting comfortable with the cattle.

This is embarrassing for a sixteen-year-old drummer and Sgt. Pepper's "head." It's a sensation that does not encourage my best behavior. Still with a wide-boy Artful Dodger accent, I decide to play my part with some confident East End swagger. This does not thrill the director. The director also writes, which complicates matters. Not surprise, he is protective of his writing and does not want his "vision" interfered with by a snotty-nosed adolescent with his head in Haight-Ashbury and his tongue lolling somewhere inside the sound of Bow Bells.

Overall, Chitty Chitty Bang Bang is an excellent choice for a seventeen-year-old who is frustrated by the restrictions of his youth. On paper, at least.

Hundreds of children from various stage schools have been sent to Pinewood to attend this casting call. There are chaperones and tutors everywhere, and everyone is doing their best to dodge them. You want to accomplish as little schoolwork as possible outside of class.

I don't recall meeting any of the cast. We were extras, so no mingling with the stars—not Dick Van Dyke, Benny Hill, or James Robertson Justice. I recall having a cyst on my forehead that was wrapped in a bandage per the doctor's directions. We kids, captives of the fearsome Child Catcher, are supposed to appear battered, bedraggled, and filthy. But in the cutting room, director Hughes notices my pristine, medically applied bandage and cuts me out of the film. Collins, please exit stage right once more.

This is another nail in the coffin of my desire for acting. And, frankly, I couldn't give a fuck. We are now in 1968, another watershed moment for music, and something must give.

I left school in the year that saw The Beatles' White Album, The Zombies' Odessey and Oracle, The Rolling Stones' Beggars Banquet, The Kinks' Village Green Preservation Society, Van Morrison's Astral Weeks, Pink Floyd's A Saucerful of Secrets, and Cream's Wheels of Fire. I hold GCEs in art, English and religious understanding. I just get by. Even if I were determined to work as an insurance salesperson in the City, I would struggle with my limited qualifications.

Such were the advantages of studying at Barbara Speake's. Throughout my time there, my head, or I, was absent. What early enthusiasm I had for the institution was mostly due to the opportunity to leave Chiswick Grammar and the promise of all those females. The school's goal was to make you a young adult theatrical star. For me, that was never going to happen, therefore I was eager to get out of it. Sure, the acting opportunities it provided pushed me out on stage in front of people, but it never seemed like a promising start to a career. But, due to financial constraints, I give acting another attempt, performing at the Piccadilly Theatre in 1969 in the previously mentioned most recent production of Oliver! (Barry Humphries is Fagin). Carol Reed's film adaption was released the previous year, and there is newfound excitement about the production. On top of that, I am now that pitiful figure: the jobbing drummer without a job as a drummer. Acting will once again require a bob or two in my pocket.

Cameron Mackintosh, who is twenty-two, is now the show's assistant stage manager. He's now arguably the most influential man in theater, an impresario with a £1 billion empire who created Les Misérables, Miss Saigon, and many more works. But in the end of the 1960s, at the Piccadilly Theatre, I was ahead of him in the pecking order. I tell him this years later, at Buckingham Palace. Sir Cameron, Sir Terry Wogan, Sir George Martin, Dame Vera Lynn, and I have been invited to meet the Queen and Prince Philip on their way to a British music festival including Jeff Beck, Jimmy Page, Eric Clapton, and Brian May.

In 1968 my focus was firmly on music. I tell Mum I want to quit acting and work as a drummer. She tells Dad. Greville Collins' youngest son is a theater and screen star, which has caused fatherly pride within the silent walls of London Assurance. But performing in one of those pop bands? In short order, I'll be a long-haired destitute raping and pillaging my way around the world, the father of a slew of illegitimate children, or worse.

Dad sends me to Coventry for weeks. He simply stops talking to me to express his outrage.

I don't mind, and I don't wobble. I have my head jammed in the back pages of Melody Maker, down the front of Lavinia's cheesecloth shirt, or occasionally both at once.

I take the life of a working drummer. Or, more specifically, I set out to identify myself as the type of person who could be considered a jobbing drummer.

One Christmas, the Caryls invite me to join a band they've formed to perform at Pontin's in Paignton, Devon. I do my best to fit in. I learn to Brylcreem my hair, tie a bow tie, wear the band jacket, and find myself dancing waltzes, rhumbas, two-steps, and a little rock'n'roll. Our repertoire includes all kinds of standards and genres.

Mrs. Caryl is a lovely lady who has a wonderful voice and a charming demeanor in front of a large crowd. Mr. Caryl is a skilled, mustachioed bandleader who knows all the tricks of the trade. He can bollock you while smiling at the audience, as he has done to me innumerable times. With a wink to the punters enjoying their chicken-in-a-basket, he'll lead the band offstage mid-set so they can quench their thirst at the bar, leaving me to entertain the crowd on my own with the little exhibition of drum trickery I have at my disposal.

"Would you like a drum solo, Phil?" "

"No! "

"It's all yours…"

At such times, I appear to have the stage to myself for an eternity. As the band raises their pint glasses in my honor, I'm desperately gesticulating for them to come back and assist me out of my pain. And gesticulating is difficult when you're holding the beat and two drumsticks.

The Charge have a profitable but risky line-up of gigs at American army sites in Norfolk and Cambridgeshire. We drive all across those counties, squeezed into a dilapidated Ford Transit, blasting the latest Motown, Stax, and James Brown classics, the faster the better. As the evening progresses, the GIs become more eager, enthused, and pissed. If you are the entertainment, you should stay onstage since it is safer. A conflict will break out at some time, according to US army regulations, therefore the longer you can keep playing and distracting them, the less likely you are to be dragged into it. The Charge perform

James Brown's locomotive rendition of "Night Train" with appropriate vigor.

I'm seventeen years old and just out of high school, but I'm quickly gaining stage presence. I also develop some leaving power, which comes in handy when The Charge's keyboard player introduces me to a friend of his named Trevor. He, too, plays keyboards, including "the pink oboe," as Peter Cook described it. Trevor frequents a Soho amusement arcade, a gay pick-up spot with additional slot machines. He informs me that The Shevelles, a popular gigging band in posh London venues, is seeking for a drummer. Dennis Elliott is leaving them and will be Foreigner's drummer.

At this point, I will pursue any and all opportunities. In The Charge, I'm a professional musician in a semi-pro band. The other guys have day jobs, but this is my day job. So my mothermust supplement my small income—perhaps a fiver each week—. She helps with the occasional backhander so I can keep my gig tickets and take out girlfriends. She is quite supportive, unlike my father, who has made a vow of silence. Nonetheless, my lack of a consistent source of income reveals an unsettling reality: I'm caught in a limbo between childhood and adulthood, between a jobless school dropout who still lives with his parents and an occasional busy drummer.

As I sit there in the buzzy gloom, waiting to jam with The Shevelles, Eric Burdon of The Animals approaches the microphone. I'm still spinning from the joy of hearing the mesmerizing voice of "House of the Rising Sun" when a lanky gentleman named Long John Baldry slips up to our table.

"Hello, Trevor," he purrs, taking a long, deliberate look at me. "Who is this? " A few minutes later, Chris Curtis, The Searchers' drummer, wanders in. He says the same thing, and I wonder whether I'm actually here for a musical audition.

Sure enough, the Shevelles leave the stage and pack up. There is no audition. Trevor tries to make up for the disappointment by inviting me back to his Kensington flat. I am skeptical, but it is late and there is a long way to the end of the line.

I return to his place. One thing leads to another—innocence turns into awkwardness. Trevor has a housemate, so I have no choice but to share his bed. Terrified, I attempt to sleep fitfully and fully clad on top of the blankets. Fidgeting begins, and a hand creeps across.

I am out of there faster than you can say "paradiddle."

Right now, I'm open to any offer. I occasionally perform with The Cliff Charles Blues Band, who are decent but not going to blow the world away, and I briefly played with The Freehold. Another jobbing band with no established talent.

This hotel is also where I meet Tony Stratton-Smith for the first time. A decade ago, as a sports journalist, he flew with Manchester United to Belgrade for a European Cup match. He missed his alarm and flight the morning after the contest. The plane crashed following a refueling stop at Munich Airport, killing twenty-three of the forty-four individuals on board, and from that point forward, Strat would always take the flight after the one that was scheduled for him.

Strat and I rapidly become fast friends, despite his insistence on calling me "Peelip." He is a fantastic and generous man who plays an important role in both my and Genesis' destiny.

My stay in The Freehold comes to an end almost as quickly as it begins, owing primarily to boredom. I press on, looking for that big break. Ronnie and I go to an audition for a band to back a British Four Tops-style outfit. We both got the gig, me on drums and Ronnie on bass, alongside a keyboardist named Brian Chatton and a guitarist named "Flash" Gordon Smith.

The four of us call ourselves Hickory. The singing group is called The Gladiators. It quickly becomes clear that the players outperform the vocalists, so we decide to split off and make a go of it on our own.

After a lot of work and some luck, it appears that I am now in a genuine band with real prospects. Suitably inspired, I attempt something I had studiously avoided till now: writing a song.

One day at home in Hounslow, I start playing the piano in the back room. I hang around D minor—which, as any Spinal Tap fan knows, is the saddest chord of all—and mull over some lyrical concepts. I am filled with phantom anguish at the idea of losing Lavinia.

I return to west London and visit Bruce Rowland. He's the son of my old elocution instructor, Hilda; a year from now, he'll play with Joe Cocker at the defining Woodstock festival before becoming the drummer for Fairport Convention. I'll buy his Gretsch drums, which I still have now.

Bruce is a drummer who is a few years older than me and definitely headed for great things. I see him daily for words of advice and support. He plays me "Loving You Is Sweeter Than Ever" by The Four Tops and tells me to "listen to the groove." Beautiful. Just amazing." He introduces me to The Grateful Dead's double live album Live Dead, which has two drummers and will play an important role in my life several years later.

We become acquainted with Brotherhood of Man, a pop group, through a friend of a friend. With a new lineup, they will win the 1976 Eurovision Song Contest with "Save Your Kisses for Me." However, in 1969, John Goodison is a member and writer. At his suggestion, we walk into a CBS Records studio and record a bland pop song called "Green Light." It's our first time in a genuine studio, and we're making a single. It seems I've finally hit the big time.

One day, two distinguished, fairly spiffily dressed elderly gentlemen arrive to see the four of us. Ken Howard and Alan Blaikley, songwriters from Hampstead, are regulars on London's swinging music scene. These movers, shakers, and ravers wrote all of the essential songs for The Herd, which features a young Peter Frampton, and Dave Dee, Dozy, Beaky, Mick, and Tich. There are numerous hits, including "The Legend of Xanadu," "Bend It," and many others. They are regulars at La Chasse, a club on Wardour Street in SoHo. It's a favorite drinking spot for musicians, located just a few doors down from the Marquee. All of the band members assemble there, crammed into a small, living-room-sized space in front of the bar—or, in the case of Keith Moon, behind it.

Moonie appears to like working as a bartender in La Chasse while he is not drumming for The Who. I buy a round from him one night, and he hands me back more money than I gave him. Another reason to love him.

Brian Chatton, Hickory's keyboardist and a very attractive Bolton man, lives in the West End and is a regular at La Chasse. Howard and Blaikley are drawn to him since they are always on the lookout for new potential.

Howard and Blaikley tell Brian one night while drinking gin and tonics that they are working on a concept album. Ark 2 is about the evacuation of a dying Earth, which is a highly topical topic in the late 1960s. Men are flying to the moon, the space race is in full swing, and many people are quite high. This rocket-powered couple has the songs; they simply need musicians to perform them. Brian does the polite thing by inviting them to see his band.

Now they're on Eel Pie Island, watching Hickory go through his paces. We're terrified to be auditioning for such well-connected gentlemen. Prior to today, my initial optimism about the band's possibilities had soon turned into pessimism—"Lying, Crying, Dying" was never more than a demo, and we appear to be going nowhere. But here are two Svengali individuals who have the power to transport us to the moon. Howard and Blaikley enjoy what they hear, and it appears that Hickory has secured the position of interstellar vehicle for their space-age music suite. We agree to board even before we hear any of the music. Their demos are, to put it mildly, crude, which is exacerbated by Howard and Blaikley's fairly awful singing voices. The material sounds florid and campy in a "rock musical" style. It merely adds to my developing skepticism—the entire "concept" strikes me as a bit schoolboyish. Next to The Who's magisterial Tommy, released in May, Ark 2 risks seeming a little, well, silly.

But we're a no-hope band who's been offered a lifeline by two guys wearing chinoiserie robes and boasting several number one songs. Hickory is sure that with Brian and Flash at the vocal helm—both

34

excellent singers—and Ronnie and I supplying a well tuned musical engine, we can take this project to the next level.

We record at De Lane Lea Studios in Holborn, under the supervision of producers Howard and Blaikley. Arranger Harold Geller is second in command and has collaborated with the team numerous times. Brian and Flash sing the majority of the songs, but I land one of the Planets Suite, a music-hall-style interlude called "Jupiter: Bringer of Jollity," and am front and center on "Space Child." Howard and Blaikley change our name to Flaming Youth, which is a phrase taken from a speech by Franklin D. Roosevelt. "Our youth's temper has become more restless, critical, and challenging. In 1936, the thirty-second President of the United States addressed the Baltimore Young Democratic Club.

Ark 2 is introduced with a PR stunt launch in London's Planetarium. The 1960s scenesters arrive two at a time. All of this ultra-fab cod-psychedelia is making me squirm; it's arrogant and ridiculous. As an assertive eighteen-year-old, I also despise Howard and Blaikley's tendency to regard us as their creation, a prefab-four totally of their making.

In Amsterdam, Howard and Blaikley show us around their favorite spots. These have their own surprises, including my first contact with a transvestite. I thought London was swinging, but it pales in comparison to Holland's party capital. Despite my reservations about the music we're forced to listen, I can't deny that Ark 2 is transporting me to intriguing new places.

Despite positive reviews and enthusiasm from the Netherlands, Ark 2 does little to improve Flaming Youth's circumstances. We rehearse till we're blue in the face, perfecting a new direction reminiscent of Yes-style orchestrated pop. But we're also a nice solid rock band that performs well on stage. However, we're performing less and less, and the shows we do play are split into two halves: one half consists of clever arrangements of interesting things—the Vanilla Fudge version of "You Keep Me Hangin' On," "With a Little Help from My Friends" à la Joe Cocker, and one of my favorite Beatles songs, "I'm Only

Sleeping," plus some of our own material—and the other half is Ark 2. The CD sounds like a wet squib when played live. The crowd is as perplexed as we are. The future viability of Flaming Youth has become a burning topic.

I can see the finish is near, so I start looking around to see what else is out there. I'll bring Ronnie along if I can find something that works for both of us. However, if the perfect drummer-only opening presents itself, I will go it alone. So far, my professional musical career, such as it is, has consisted of my saying yes to every opportunity, only to be disappointed with the results. It's time for a more aggressive approach.

I became a professional auditioner, always perusing the "musicians wanted" ads in the back pages of Melody Maker. If the advertisement is present, the act retains some integrity. I try out unsuccessfully for Vinegar Joe, the future home of Robert Palmer and Elkie Brooks. I am unable to impress Manfred Mann Chapter Three, serial bandleader Mann's jazz-rock experimentalists. I even try it with The Bunch, a functional but unremarkable band based in Bournemouth.

I've taken a risk and put myself out there. When Yes performs at the Marquee in front of fifty hardy folks, I go backstage during the intermission because I have heard Bill Bruford is returning to Leeds University. Frontman Jon Anderson gave me his phone number, but I never called. I'm not sure why, but I often wonder what my life would be like if I had said yes to the Yes audition.

As the 1970s arrive, marking the end of my first year of adulthood, I'm searching for food, money, and a future. I've been in a few bands, none of them have resulted in anything. I'm hungry, yet I'm still stranded in Hounslow, with all that comes with being at the end of the line. The fact that I am currently alone at home adds to the emptiness of my existence.

While my life has been moving forward, there have been some significant changes at 453 Hanworth Road. To put it bluntly, everyone has left, and the Collins family has split. Clive and Carole have their own adult lives, and my parents' relationship has come to a halt. Mum has started spending more time at Barbara Speake's place, closer to work. Dad is looking forward to retirement and growing a beard. He is a frequent visitor to Weston-super-Mare and spends extended weekends there. It's a town he grew to love during the war, when his family was evacuated by London Assurance and he was stationed there as a member of Dad's Army's local Home Guard detachment.

So, while I technically have a place to live, my spirit has no permanent residence.

I had to get out of this place. But how?

Then a Beatle throws me a bone.

Chapter 4: The Ballad of All Things Must Pass

When opportunity knocks, I'm just getting out of the bathtub in the house where I grew up. It's a peaceful Thursday afternoon; I spend most of my time alone in the otherwise vacant Collins family home, and all I have to look forward to is Top of the Pops on television and beans on toast for tea. I might watch TV and eat dinner in my underwear. Because I can. It's May 1970, I'm nineteen, and the swinging sixties have officially finished. Bring on the soggy seventies.

Still, I am a small star in Ken Howard and Alan Blaikley's orbit. They're friendly with Martin, another acquaintance from La Chasse who happens to be Ringo Starr's chauffeur. One night at the club, Martin asks Blaikley whether he knows any decent percussion players. He doesn't say much about the musician who will be presenting the session, but the mention of Abbey Road has me intrigued. No matter who it is. I can see where the Beatles recorded. McCartney announced his departure from the band just weeks ago, and his debut solo album, McCartney, has just been released. Everyone is talking about the Fab Four ending. Let It Be, The Beatles' final single, has only just hit the shelves, yet the music press is already buzzing about the first post-Beatles solo album.

But thinking on my feet, soaked in my towel, my thoughts isn't going there. At this juncture in my stop-start, still-emerging music career, this is an opportunity to show off my drumming abilities to an artist talented enough to be hired at Abbey Road. I am a jobless drummer, and this is a job.

"What time do you want me there?"

I dress for the event, which includes a T-shirt over pants. I am a nineteen-year-old with long hair, and this is how I look. I call a cab, get in, and am overjoyed to be able to say the iconic phrase: "Abbey Road, please, driver."

When I arrive, Martin, the chauffeur, is standing on the steps of the studio in St. John's Wood, northwest London. "Come in, come in, we've been waiting for you."

"Really? Me?" I'm wondering. "And who's this 'we' he's referring to?" He greets me and we exchange light talk. "They've been here four weeks," he explains. "They've spent one thousand pounds. And they didn't record anything."

I am thinking, "Wow, this must be serious."

Everyone stops talking as I enter. I'm receiving a collective inquisitive frown: Who is this kid?

Chauffeur Martin says, "The percussionist is here."

I'm not sure what my expected position is in the events, but "percussionist" sounds good to me, even if I don't actually consider myself that. Anyway, there's no time to argue, because George is now speaking to me: "Sorry, man," he says in that classic Scouse drawl, "you haven't been here long enough to be in the photograph." I giggle awkwardly, slightly ashamed.

Back down the stairs, Mal Evans, with his huge glasses and early moptop fringe haircut—even The Beatles' roadies were heroes—directs me to my location. "Here's your congas, kid, next to Ringo's drums."

I'm looking at the drums. I want to touch those drums. Feel the drums. If I felt I could get away with resting my cheek on the skins, I would have done so. How does Ringo mic his kit? Ooh, towel over the snare—that's intriguing.

Anyway, Abbey Road on a Thursday evening in late spring/early summer 1970. I have my congas, Ringo on my right, and Billy Preston on my left. George and Klaus are somewhere there. We're planning to record a song titled "Art of Dying."

"Well, shall we play Phil the song first?" Nobody says that. Not George, Ringo, or Spector. Something else no one says: "Phil, here's the sheet music. That's how it works, and that's where you come in. George does not come and do this. He does not hand me anything. He's there, doing his thing, putting his thoughts together, whatever.

Soon, I'll be chain smoking. I take a couple from Billy and a few from Ringo. I don't feel great, and it's not just because I'm fast puffing my way through the better part of a packet. I sense I'm getting on everyone's nerves. Years later, I was scheduled to deliver a gong to

Ringo at the Mojo Awards, and I had a pack of Marlboros ready for him. Unfortunately, I became sick and couldn't attend the event. So I still owe Ringo those cigarettes.

This is probably how he made those beautiful records. And whenever he says "drums," I play. I'd rather err on the side of caution than risk having the notoriously volatile (and trigger-happy) Spector yell at me, "Why aren't you playing, man?" So I keep playing. Because I'm not a percussionist and am nervous, I probably overplay. So I'm giving it. After an hour, my hands are in a state. Red, raw, blistering. I'd have comparable session experiences years later with Elton John's chosen percussionist, Ray Cooper, a fantastic player who can really push it, and then push it some more. There was blood on the walls. No surprise Elton adores him.

After a dozen takes, I still haven't been requested to play anything in particular. So I just played what I felt was suitable. I just keep playing, and playing. All this time, I haven't had any feedback from Spector, which is a little concerning. But I'm simply trying to blend in, look cool, and avoid dropping the ball or the beat.

I'm standing there, gazing at my wounded hands, probably dizzy from all the cigarettes, and thinking, "Spector, you bastard." "My hands are completely shot, and you haven't even listened to me."

Billy and Ringo, positioned on each side of me, chuckle. They are clearly concerned for me. They know how hard I've worked, and they must understand how nervous this adolescent child is. He must have been very apprehensive throughout the evening. To be so optimistic and then to be brutally shot down.

But it breaks the ice, so we play it a couple more times. Then everyone disappears. Just like that. I leave and contact Lavinia from the pay phone in the foyer. "You will never guess where I am. Abbey Road! "With the Beatles!" What I'm actually saying is, "I can't believe my fucking luck. You're definitely going to want to get frisky with me after this!" Sore hands? Why are my hands sore?

A few weeks later, I receive the payment in the mail. It's from EMI, costs £15, and is for services rendered to Mr. George Harrison during the production of the album All Things Must Pass. I would have kept the check as a souvenir if I hadn't needed it so severely.

The next step is pre-order the album. I visit my neighborhood record store, Memory Discs, in Hounslow. "I'd like to order the George Harrison CD All Things Must Pass. "I'm on it, you know?" I do not say that. I do not think I said it. But I wouldn't have put it past me.

The phone finally rings in late November, after an agonizing wait. "Hello, Mr. Collins?" It's a memory disc. "Your record is in." Yes, this is my record. Finally, it's available for purchase.

This is a terrible letdown. I am devastated. Then I perk up. Oh well, I'll just go home and listen. If I can't see myself on the sleeve, I can at least hear myself in the grooves. But as soon as the needle strikes the record and the music begins, I realize I'm not on "Art of Dying." They haven't even used the arrangement I worked on. Oh, my God. What's happening?

At this point, I am unfamiliar with the concept of recording different versions of songs. Yes, I had created Ark 2 with Flaming Youth. But, aside from that, I'm a young shaver who has barely been in any recording studios, let alone the world's most famous recording studio, with the world's most famous American producer, and two Beatles. I had no idea Phil Spector considered various arrangements meat and potatoes. "We're gonna have to abort last week's session, I gotta new idea…"

I went from flying high to crashing low.

That type of encounter, that confirmation, is extremely essential to me. Forget Oliver! and the fact that I was registered with an agency as a serious child actor. I may have been a contender, but acting did not interest me. All I want to be is a drummer, and I've planned my life accordingly: pop for the time being, followed by The Ray McVay Show Band every Friday and Saturday at the Lyceum. Maybe some recording sessions, and if I can learn to read music, the orchestra pit.

One day in 1982, I'm working at The Farm with Gary Brooker of Procol Harum on his Lead Me to the Water record. Gary poses the question: "Should we get Eric or George to play guitar?" Gary has spent the last few years in Clapton's touring band, and he knows Harrison—he also performed on All Things Must Pass, but his piano performance made the cut.

So, because he can, Gary invites both to play guitar, and they both accept. When George arrives, I introduce myself. "Yeah, George, we've actually met before..." I begin, and then tell him about that May evening in Abbey Road twelve years ago.

"Really, Phil?" "I don't recall that at all."

Brilliant. A Beatles ruined my life, and I remember nothing about it. If I was feeling sick earlier...

At least George sets my mind at ease about another issue. Rumors circulated that I was going to join his old friend McCartney in Wings. The whispers were not true despite sounding intriguing. George quickly assures me that it was not a gig I would have chosen. Being the fifth drummer for Wings would have been "a fate worse than death."

In 1999, I attend the sixtieth birthday party of Formula One racing ace Jackie Stewart. I met Jackie in the '80s, and we got along great. Jackie would take me clay pigeon shooting, which was not my thing, and I'd get him tickets to see Genesis and invite his sons Paul and Mark to my shows.

I bought Jackie's house in Switzerland in 1996, which cemented our connection even more. So by the end of the 1990s, when he launches Stewart Grand Prix with son Paul, we've become great friends. I've never gone to a Grand Prix, but George and Eric are great motor racing fans. So, my wife Orianne and I have been invited to these delightful weekends in Hockenheim, where we will meet Schumacher, Coulthard, Barrichello, and the rest of the great Formula One drivers. The actual race day is almost like a sideshow because there is nothing to see at a Grand Prix. You'd be better off sitting in a caravan and watching it on television. However, practice and qualifying are both enjoyable. High-speed hospitality at its best.

So here we are at Jackie's birthday party in his new property in the United Kingdom, near the Prime Minister's weekend hideaway,

Chequers, in Buckinghamshire. There are many high rollers, royalty, and racecar racers in attendance. I'm seated at a table with Princess Anne's children, Zara and Peter. Also present and correct is George.

Perhaps, thirty years later, I should finally take George's solo masterwork at its word. Everything must pass, including my rejection from one of the best albums ever.

I think, "This is it. "Somewhere on this tape..." It's almost as if I'm carrying the Holy Grail (of teenage conga sessions). "I did not dream it. And it's not like George found it in that Tokyo record shop known for having every Fab Four bootleg ever. Because I have checked that shop and it wasn't there. "George himself has sent me this."

I don't listen to it right away. I cannot bring myself to. But soon, I walk somberly into my home studio. I shut the door, pull up a chair, insert the tape, and hit play. Suddenly, there is a hiss, and the drums begin. Ba-da-dad, doom!

Then the sound of congas explodes from the speakers. To educated ears, the flaws of the wincingly arrhythmic cacophony are obvious. Christ Almighty! Turn it off.

A hyperactive child had been wild. You can tell the player has some talent because his performance isn't wholly random. But it's everywhere, and someone in charge says, "Get rid of that kid!"

I'm in shock. I can't recall it being this horrible. My playing is overly busy, frantic, and amateurish. Clearly, this was not what Messrs Harrison and Spector required.

Suddenly, the truth emerged. All these years, I had hoped that the tune would take a different musical route. With that notion, I consoled myself and calmed my thirty-year-old disappointment. And now I understand: I was fired. They did not disappear to watch football or do drugs. They were getting rid of me. Someone said, "Lose the youngster conga player. We are fading." As you would if you didn't know what to say, especially if famous rock stars surrounded you. You escape, leaving Chauffeur Martin to do the dirty work and abandoning the nineteen-year-old.

I eventually see the hilarious side, especially after George verifies that, to the best of his knowledge, I was not dismissed.

George wrote fresh sleeve notes for the booklet accompanying the thirtieth anniversary edition, which was issued in March 2001, seven months before his death. "I don't remember it, but apparently a teenage Phil Collins was there…"

George, bless him, sent me a remixed CD reissue. It's fantastic, albeit it would be tremendously improved by including "my" version of "Art of Dying."

I still have the comic congas tape. It is one of my possessions. Here's to you, George—the wonderful bastard.

Chapter 5: The Genesis of Genesis

Spring has blossomed into summer 1970, and I can characterize my mood as both flourishing and wilting. On the positive side, I've just been to Abbey Road with two Beatles and have raw, blistered fingers and hands to prove it. At this point, I consider myself a member of All Things Must Pass' all-star recording cast. Despite his shaky hands, that's probably as excellent as it gets for a nineteen-year-old drummer with twitchy ambition in his sticks.

On the downside, Flaming Youth are at best smoldering. Ark 2 had established the controls for the sun's heart, but had returned to Earth. I know I'm a talented player, but I can't picture George Harrison inviting me to join his touring band. I require a full-time job, a better job, or preferably both.

Every Thursday, I rush to my local newsagent and pick up the entire week's music papers. Like every sports fan, I begin reading from the back. I sift through the job postings, discarding those that do not fit: "Skiffle quartet seeks percussionist." Must have personal washboard and teeth"; "Country band seeks quiet drummer wearing cowboy hat." I also look through concert listings to discover which groups have the most bookings. I'm hoping to prevent another rehearsal-room band like Flaming Youth has become. I want to go out and play with people other than ourselves.

One of the reasons I'm interested is the mention of Stratton-Smith. I knew him from hanging out at the Russell Hotel with The Freehold. Since then, he's had some success managing The Koobas, a Liverpool beat group, and Hertfordshire rock band The Creation, whose singles "Making Time" and "Painter Man" were both major hits. I also know he founded his own record label, Charisma.

I call my old friend Ronnie Caryl. I believe that presenting ourselves as a package at this audition will increase our chances of landing the job. He doesn't have much expertise on the 12-string, but he's a brilliant player and should be able to summon the necessary skills. Ronnie, like me, is looking for a way out of Flaming Youth.

After some furrowed brow map-reading and a couple of false turns down country lanes, we arrive at the address given to us. Ronnie drives the Morris Minor up an appropriately gritty gravel driveway, and we park up outside a big, lovely country pile. Our guitars and drums appear to spill out of the car, making the entire scenario look a lot less orderly. I'm suddenly self-conscious about my attire. My worn-in flares and T-shirt appear a touch underdressed for this occasion. I ring the bell, and after what seems like an eternity, a distinguished-looking, middle-aged woman opens the door. Mrs. Gabriel eventually realizes that we are not here to sell Encyclopaedia Britannica or join her bridge group. We must be here to audition for her son's pop group.

"Oh, do come in," she adds with a smile. "You are a little early. Please feel free to have a swim while you wait.

I think, "Wow, trees and a swimming pool." Things are looking up. If only I had remembered to bring my swim trunks to this rock'n'roll audition. But, trunks or not, I decide to take the plunge. If there's one thing I've learned over the previous few years, it's to take advantage of every opportunity. Who knows if I'll ever again be offered a swim in a private heated pool in the countryside. I casually peel off my jeans, leaving only my graying Y-fronts, and jump in. The pool seems wonderful. This is first-class luxury.

The only thing missing is a Sobranie inhaled via a cigarette holder. He's young-looking but beautifully easygoing, the type of guy you aspire to be when you grow up. But, if this is Peter Gabriel's father, how young is Gabriel?

A grand piano has been brought onto the terrace, and another man is loitering in the shadows, ready to play it. He introduces himself as Anthony Banks, Genesis' twenty-year-old keyboardist. My first impressions? I don't actually have any. Tony is reserved to the point of invisibility, another politely spoken young guy who will not say boo to a goose—unless, as I soon discover, that goose plays the wrong chord.

Finally, I met Peter Gabriel. He's twenty years old and shares the same high standards as his bandmates. His demeanor can be described as hesitating, with one hand grasping the other arm at the elbow, nearly shy, very humiliated, and don't-look-at-me- I'm-not-here. He is in command—well, his parents are, as it is their home—but he does not want to be perceived as in charge.

Peter and Tony met at Charterhouse in 1963, and Mike joined a year later. Genesis founded in 1967 from two student bands, with Anthony Phillips on guitar and Chris Stewart on drums. That year, Jonathan King, an Old Carthusian with some success in the music industry, became the five-piece's "manager," landing them a record deal with Decca.

Genesis reformed in the summer of 1969, after all members had graduated, to discuss a second album. Before they could do it, they lost another drummer, Silver, who was replaced by John Mayhew. He was an occasional carpenter seeking for a drumming gig when Mike found his phone number. Genesis debuted in September 1969 at a teenager's birthday party. Now that they were fully committed to the band, they proceeded to rehearse and perform wherever and whenever possible. It's no surprise that their name appeared repeatedly in Melody Maker. Tony Stratton-Smith visited them in the spring of 1970, midway through a six-week tenure at Upstairs at Ronnie's, Ronnie Scott's Jazz Club in Soho. He quickly signed them to a management and recording contract with Charisma.

Genesis began recording their second album, Trespass, in June in Soho's Trident Studios, with producer John Anthony on board. However, in July, before the album's release, Ant Phillips announced his departure. He became ill due to overwork and performance fright. Cue that Melody Maker advertisement from July 1970, by which point Tony, Mike, and Peter had been through a lot in their seven years of friendship and music producing. They have specific procedures and expectations, and specific ways of interacting with one another.

It will take me a long to grasp these dynamics. Tony and Peter, for example, are best friends and worst foes. Tony is prone to loosing his temper, but this really becomes obvious later, when Peter and Tony take turns storming out of the studios in a fury.

Similarly, I don't know how close they've gotten to splitting, and thus how much depends on these auditions. I'm also not aware that Genesis' carefully balanced creative symmetry has been thrown out from under it. Previously, Genesis had two pairs of writers: Mike and Ant and Tony and Peter. Then there were three.

So today's mood at Gabriel's is fragile and tense. Also frighteningly guarded, highly strung, a touch rarefied, and extremely uptight. In summary, nothing resembles myself or my past. What could possible go right?

But we all have one thing in common: we are all talented musicians.

Right now, however, Ronnie and I are unaware of these subtleties and undercurrents. We're seated in a massive living room, made even more spacious by the absence of the grand piano, with a few other disoriented hopes. It is now hiding under a massive umbrella on the terrace next to the swimming pool. The image is a still-life inspired by Dalí and Storm Thorgerson, reminiscent of a prog-rock record sleeve from the 1970s.

We perform three or four songs, including Trespass' epic closer "The Knife," and some acoustic sections, to test how sensitive I am to acoustic music.

I'm the final drummer that day, and I'm trying to figure out how well—or not—I've done. To no avail. These are tightly wound English public schoolboys, and reserve and politesse are their primary combat abilities. They will, they say gravely, "let me know."

I subsequently discover that Peter knew I was the guy the moment I sat down. It appears that the confident way I put up my kit was telling. Mike was less convinced. Tony felt quietly confident. Mrs. Gabriel's opinions are not recorded in history.

On August 8, 1970, the phone rings on the red leatherette and white wrought-iron phone bench at 453 Hanworth Road. A voice I'll get used to over the next five years says down a crackly phone line, "Er, um, ah, hello, Phil?" It's Peter Gabriel here. From Genesis. You have the job, if you want it."

"Yeah, Peter, thanks a lot."

I attempt to be cool, but inside I'm bouncing. I finally discovered a band, or rather, a band found me. Finally, I'm going to play drums in front of people. It does not get better than that.

First things first. I call Ronnie.

"Seems like I got the job with Genesis."

"Oh yes. Did they mention anything about me?

"Ah, no…"

"Fuck! "I suppose I was a little too bluesy for them anyway...

Ronnie's disappointment is reasonable, and it will be long-lasting. He will attend all of Genesis' London gigs to support his old friend, but he will also slag us off. It becomes a routine component of the post-show: drink, rant, critique, and declaration of lifelong friendship.

In desperate need of money, particularly to take Lavinia out, I feel compelled to take advantage of our most recent round of "going steady": I ask her father if he has any work. Fred Lang, a builder and handyman, is now working on a major exterior decoration project in Wembley. I exchange my drumsticks for a paintbrush, grateful but humiliated. Rock 'n' roll and my role in its future will have to wait a little longer.

The work comprises repainting all of the windows and wooden parts on the exterior of this poor unknowing couple's home. The painting is the easiest part. The preparation—removing the old paint and preparing the bare wood—kills you. Because old paint is sometimes lead-based, it might literally kill you.

As an excitable and angry teenager and aspiring musician, I have no patience for tedious tasks like peeling old paint, especially outside in a cold, damp English summer. The meticulous polish that I will eventually apply to my demos and even my model trains does not exist here. This is terrible because finesse is exactly what is necessary for this task. But somehow I manage to pull the wool over Fred's eyes and pretend that this preparation went perfectly, allowing me to complete the final stage of painting.

I'm pretty good at slopping on paint. Over the padlock on the garden shed, over the door locks, over the window frames—it goes haphazardly and randomly. Sure, the straight lines around the windows leave something to be desired. But by the time the flaws in my work are apparent, I'll be far away. It never occurred to me that messing up at my girlfriend's father's workplace would not be the best idea a hopeful young suitor could have.

After the longest two weeks in history, Peter, Mike, and Tony return from vacation. Mike invites me to stay at his parents' house in Farnham because they all live in Surrey and I live in far-flung west London. It's another huge property, but with a very friendly, homey atmosphere. I happily leave London and move in with Mike, vowing never to pick up a paintbrush again for the rest of my life.

The rest of my life begins with Genesis' new lineup's first rehearsals in September 1970, amid the pigeon-shit-encrusted confines of the Maltings, an old, barn-like facility in Farnham. We set up our gear and begin playing with what I can only characterize as hazy enthusiasm: other public-school buddies of Peter, Tony, and Mike drop in, I discover exotic new snacks like Marmite and tahini, and the entire operation is frequently enveloped in the sweet fragrance of grass.

Richard MacPhail remains a constant presence. He sang in The Anon, one of Charterhouse's pre-Genesis bands. He's the road manager, sound engineer, and a major pothead. Maybe he has to be, as he sleeps in the Maltings, sharing a berth with the pigeons and their guano while guarding the equipment. He introduces me to the pleasures of stoned headphone use. Crosby, Stills, and Nash's Déjà Vu is about to be released, and Richard brings out the album, builds a massive joint, and orders Mike and me to immerse ourselves in the auditory beautiful harmonies of "Carry On." It's not quite kicking open the doors of perception, but I'm pounding softly.

Do I feel like an oik? Certainly, a bit. But I already know I can contribute something to Genesis. Something that is needed. Not simply in terms of musical ability, however I am aware that with my drumming, I can make that blancmange as hard as we require.

I'm also quick to crack a joke, which will come in good when Peter, Mike, and Tony resume schoolyard bickering. When they start squabbling about who took whose protractor, I can always intervene with some distracting chitchat. My charisma and ability to break the ice are just what these buttoned-up public schoolboys require, even if they don't realize it. English reserve will only get you so far. In the same way that my limited expertise as a songwriter means I'll be the band's musical arranger in these early days, I can also change the tone. All things considered, this is my ideal work. Genesis is a busy, well-known band with a record deal. Also, I like these dudes. They are interesting. There's no twelve-bar blues here. We are different, but have much in common. I can make this work. I can absolutely fit into these trousers.

Chapter 6: From Blue Boar to Fox's Head

Our chemistry is immediately evident during rehearsals in Maltings. It's a nice old barn where we like performing, improvising, and writing. Performance will test this experimental lineup. Or, more accurately, travel for performance. How will the combustible components of the "new" Genesis interact in the more regulated environment of a small, wheezing, British-made family car?

Our objectives were far greater than those of rural Surrey, and we spent the latter months of 1970 touring the country in Peter's Hillman Imp or Mike's Mini Traveller. However, old habits die hard, and a hierarchy emerges quickly. Unsurprisingly, I finish last.

Being the driver puts you in prime position. It indicates you have control, and you can use all of your Green Shield stamps when you fill up with gas. Peter and Mike will proudly acquire a 24-piece dinner service before I even see a saucer.

When Peter is driving, Tony usually wins the dispute about who should sit in the passenger seat. The rest of us crowd into the back, competing for space with a variety of electric and acoustic guitars.

For a while, "the rest of us" referred to three of us, as there is another guitarist, Mick Barnard. Following Ronnie's unsuccessful audition, we continued as a four-piece, with Tony attempting to play all of the guitar parts on a Hohner electric piano through a fuzzbox. Then we found Mick. He's a lovely person and a talented guitarist, but he doesn't last. My lasting impression of Mick's brief time in Genesis is not his playing or anything musical, but the fact that we always dropped him off after shows at Toddington Services on the M1 near Dunstable, Bedfordshire. I have no idea how he got home from there.

Stopping at the Blue Boar facilities near Watford Gap on the M1 is one of the unexpected ways romance manifests itself. Many bands stop there on their way back from shows in the north. An early-morning meal of beans on toast and an inter-band rant against the kids at Leeds University are exactly the thing for footsore rockers. And from this moment on, you can see the light: up until now, it's been unending cat's eyes on the road. However, from Watford Gap, the motorway has overhead lights to direct you south and homeward. In the absence of speed or other medications, that will be the only wake-up call we get. When Peter drives, he speaks. We'll be bombing up the M1 toward the Midlands, and you'll notice this high-pitched whine. It's not me grumbling in the back about a lack of Green Shield stamps. It's Peter, driving 80 mph in second gear. He's so caught up in what he's trying to communicate that he forgot to shift gears. He eventually shifts, and the automobile relaxes.

There's a Christmas tree of plugs packed into a socket that, in the darkness, I trip on and kick out. All the stage power goes out, and everything falls apart: lights, sound, and atmosphere. I flee quickly before the now-subatomic headliners see me.

However, gigs are usually professionally run. Get there, get on, and get back. There are a few joints, but no raucous bacchanalia. The closest we get is a show at London's City University, which also happens to be Steve's first Genesis gig. Our stage time is later than indicated, so I pass the time by drinking some Newcastle Browns. By the time we get onstage, I'm all over the place. I execute all the proper fills, but three inches to the right of each drum. Forget air guitar; this is air drums. Afterward, I'm wincing: "What must this new guitarist think?" "First gig, and the drummer is furious." That was my first time playing intoxicated, and it will be the last.

The tour is a resounding success, establishing all three bands as huge, arena-filling performers. The NME describes the scenes in Newcastle: "Well over 500 people had to be left out in the cold while 2500 enthusiasts created scenes of almost unparallel [sic] hysteria in the sanctum of City Hall." In Manchester, the Free Trade Hall "had crocodiles of long-haired youths surrounding it for the last remaining tickets."

It's also fantastic fun behind the scenes, with plenty of Newcastle Brown-fueled merriment on the shared tour bus that takes us over the country. I join Alan Hull and the Lindisfarne boys—hearty Geordies to a man—and share a cigarette or three with the road crew. But for

Genesis as a whole, there may be too much merriment: this is our first bus tour, and it will be our last. Buses go far slower than vehicles, and journeys often last much longer than necessary. According to the AA guide, the journey from London to Newcastle is 274 miles long and takes forever by coach. So we decide to go our own way and then return to our own forms of transportation: Peter's Hillman Imp and Mike's Mini Traveller.

Genesis has made significant inroads in Belgium. After my trip to the Netherlands with Flaming Youth, all I need now is some love from Luxembourg, and I can certainly say I am popular in Benelux.

So, in March 1971, Genesis performs their first foreign show at Ferme Cinq, a small bar in Charleroi. We take the cross-Channel ferry, and when we arrive, our enthusiasm at being an international touring band is heightened when we find that the stage is made of beer crates. We must place them properly so that they do not wobble and tumble during the odd, neo-fantasy discourse. We miraculously stay upright and go down like a storm. Each of the half-dozen shows is the same: packed and spectacular. Genesis has taken off, finally. In Belgium, at any rate.

At home, we're still playing at Farx, a club within a pub in Potters Bar, and another Farx on Uxbridge Road in Southall. The latter is one of the few performances my father visits, as it is close to Barbara Speake's house, where my mother lives, and not far from Hounslow, where he is spending his final few months before moving to Weston-super-Mare permanently.

However, my sole recollection is of him really attending. No additional details emerge; I have no recollection of Dad saying, "Good job, son." Perhaps he waited just long enough to drink a half-pint of bitters. I assume he still thinks I'm not worth much. It's just a tavern, and his youngest child appears to be part of a musical ensemble with little musicianship that dad understands. Around this time, it is not uncommon for us to play tunes with no lyrics, songs that are clearly incomplete, and/or Peter to sing meaningless words.

Ironically, this is also the point at which my true blood ties are stretched to their limits. In June, Mum and Dad make the decision to sell 453 Hanworth Road. But in the summer of 1971, a year after I joined Genesis, band life marches on inexorably, distractingly, and we decamp to Luxford House in Crowborough, East Sussex. It's Strat's leased home, and his suggestion: bands "getting it together in the country"—that is, creating songs away from the hustle and bustle of the city—is very much the in-thing. If it's okay for Traffic and Led Zeppelin, it's fine for Genesis.

The house is a stunning Tudor mansion with a decent outbuilding suitable for composing sessions. We have delicious meals provided by one of the roadies, drink red wine by the barrel, and head to the sweeping lawns to play croquet. This old-fashioned, upper-crust, very English game inspires the jacket image for the upcoming album Nursery Cryme. Personally, I think the pictures by Paul Whitehead (who also did Trespass) are a little off. But I was outvoted, and he will also design the artwork for our next album, Foxtrot.

When it comes to selecting rooms at Luxford House, the pecking order again comes into play. Pete, Mike, and Tony get to choose their sleeping arrangements first, followed by Steve and I.

Finally, I'm not troubled because there are more essential things to consider—this will be Genesis' debut album with the new lineup. Our novels are "The Fountain of Salmacis" together with "The Return of the Giant Hogweed." I'm in my element, enjoying the creative freedom, the flow of ideas, the scope of our ambition, and the length of our songs. I feel confident and emancipated, and the boys have encouraged me to contribute.

There is also room to maneuver. Some composing sessions have us gathering around Tony, who is sitting at his Hammond organ, with Mike playing 12-string guitar and Peter improvising vocals. I will improvise alongside him. Similarly, Peter writes "Harold the Barrel" on piano as I stand alongside him, singing harmony and contributing ideas. I can pound out a few piano chords, but my insecurity says, "They've heard this all before!" One thing I've learned from writing with the boys is never to accept the first melody concept you come up with. Dig deeper and experiment with it. Explore. When you listen to The Beatles' "She Loves You," the chord sequence is incredibly simple, but the melody they add on top of that simplicity is brilliantly created. I pick up all of the tips and tactics from Peter, Mike, and Tony, who are far more seasoned writers than I am.

Since then, on every Genesis album, every vocal other than Peter's on backgrounds and harmonies is mine. The other boys aren't particularly talented singers. But I am content to sing in the background, from the comfort of my stool.

Nursery Cryme, recorded in Soho's Trident with John Anthony, who produced Trespass, will be released in November 1971. It reached number four in Italy, becoming the second European country to adopt Genesis. We play in the Italian capital's Palazzetto dello Sport, an arena built for the 1960 Olympics that can accommodate 3,500 sitting Romans and 10,000 standing, and they adore us.

This is the largest venue we've ever played in, and we plan to continue doing so for many years. Italian audiences are extraordinary. They not only love us deeply, they "get" it. They whoop and praise even a shift in mood, which Genesis excels at—we can go from up-tempo to murmured nothing to pastoral interlude with simply a toss of our hair. It's no surprise that the Italians are so passionate about us: we're an English band that has tapped into the operatic tradition.

It's a reciprocal love affair that will culminate thirty years later, in 2007, when Genesis wraps up the first part of the Turn It On Again reunion tour with a free concert at Circo Massimo (Circus Maximus) in front of an estimated half-million spectators. As a Roman history buff, I consider a place where chariots formerly raced for the Emperor's entertainment to be the pinnacle of maximus rock'n'roll.

I'm gone from Una Billings for a few hours one day, and when I return, Tony, Mike, and Steve had played around with a 9/8 riff. I have no idea what is going on, so I just start playing. I alternate between playing with the riff and joining Tony. I'm still quite pleased of the final recorded performance of the piece, which became "Apocalypse in 9/8," which shows me making it up as I go.

Most importantly, Tony, Mike, and Peter deserve credit for recognizing that all of those components could come together to form more than just five songs strung together across twenty-three minutes. Nonetheless, we're concerned about "Supper's Ready" fitting on the album: the more music on a vinyl LP, the shallower the grooves and the lower the volume will be. Twenty-three minutes is testing the limits of one side of a 33-rpm long-player. Worse, most individuals in 1972 had an eight-track cassette in their automobile, which faded in and out three or four times. It's absurd to consider such physical constraints on music.

As a result, Genesis is actually pushing the limits of what bands can accomplish on one album. Tubular Bells was the only other similarly ambitious and substantial piece of music available at the time. Since its release seven months after Foxtrot, we've been playing Mike Oldfield's pioneering debut over the PA system at our shows. It serves to energize the audience before we take the stage, and to help us plan our preparations. We'd know where we were based on a specific section. "Oh, it's 'Bagpipe Guitars,' boys, time to get dressed!"

Performing "Supper's Ready" presents unique obstacles. The first dozen or so times we execute it, including its debut at Brunel University on November 10, 1972, the five of us are continually attempting to catch up with one another, such is the focus required to perform a long piece of music. However, it is a hit with our audiences from the start, and we always feel relieved when we reach the finish. Especially if we finish at the same time. If if it was the only challenge we faced onstage.

On September 19, 1972, the month before Foxtrot's release, we're scheduled to play at Dublin's National Stadium. I'm anxious about playing in this 2,000-capacity boxing venue. It's our first trip in Ireland, and I'm afraid we're pushing our luck at a venue of this size and type.

But we roll onstage and go right into the set. We are now in the instrumental section of Nursery Cryme's opening tune, "The Musical Box," which is quite lengthy. Long enough to wear a dress.

Prior to this, there had been no indication that Peter was considering a new fancy-dress path. Moving forward, there is no mention of the flower mask he will wear for the "Willow Farm" section of "Supper's Ready," or the triangular box head he will wear for the following piece, "Apocalypse in 9/8." We see none of it before the audience does. He will not entertain any suggestions for a band choice. He believes that such democracy in theatrical things will merely drag down the process and lead to discussions about what color the outfit should be and whether the flower is a hardy annual or a perennial.

It's almost the end of 1972, and I have no notion that Dad is ill. He's relocated entirely to Weston and rarely visits London. But 453 Hanworth Road has finally been sold. It marks the end of an era, and my life must continue. I begin renting a wet flat in Downs Avenue, Epsom, in a hastily restored, decaying Georgian home. The walls are paper thin, and when it rains, the interior is just as wet as the outside.

In December 1972, we perform our first two American gigs. Our arrival in the new world is not particularly auspicious. We arrive to discover that our U.S. manager, Ed Goodgold, who also manages Woodstock legends Sha Na Na, has booked us a gig at Brandeis University near Boston, Massachusetts. At noon. So our first performance on American territory is an unceremonious, crashing failure. New England students appear to be less interested in English rock bands than we had previously imagined, instead focusing on their studies or sandwiches. This does not speak well for Genesis' future in the United States of America.

We're overwhelmed as we approach New York for the first time, the sheer immensity of the city pressing down on a band whose heads have already bent following Boston's letdown. Driving in over the George Washington Bridge at dark, the Manhattan skyline comes to life, lighted by millions of lights. New York! We saw it in the movies, and now we're here.

My senses whirling from the sight of steam rising from sewer vents, the scent of pretzels roasting, the constant honking of yellow cabs, and the euphoric views down the canyons of steel, my first visit to New York will stay with me no matter how many times I return.

We check into our hotel, The Gorham, an arty, slightly run-down establishment in Midtown near Fifth Avenue. We explore briefly before falling asleep. The next day, we shoot some promotional images in Central Park and outside the famed Greenwich Village venue, The Bitter End. Then it's off to the Philharmonic Hall for our soundcheck, when we uncover a huge issue: the unusual power system in the United States means that the motored instruments run on sixty cycles rather than fifty, as they do in the United Kingdom. This means the Mellotron (a new instrument we got from King Crimson) and Hammond organ are out of sync with the guitars.

We find a workaround and get through our show that night. The audience doesn't seem to notice anything amiss, but despite the five of us being telepathically in sync, Genesis' performance is a disaster. We walk offstage, take the lift up to the dressing room, and the air is blue with wrath. Even years later, the memory of this first New York event sends everyone into a frenzy as all of the awful memories flood back. However, all things considered, I travel back to the United Kingdom on a high. So Genesis' first trip to America was not wholly successful—at least I was there, which not many people I knew in 1972 could claim.

Dad dies on Christmas Day at 8 a.m.

To be honest, I'm probably too preoccupied to be upset (that comes later), even as my brother describes my father's deplorable living conditions: so much damp that it was visible all down the walls of the small cottage he was living in—a terribly unhealthy environment, especially for someone with heart problems. He most certainly had diabetes, and when he came at the hospital, doctors considered amputating both of his legs. Mum and Clive agreed that Dad would have preferred not to live if something had happened to him.

Dad's funeral is on January 1, 1973. I am in a daze. I recall the casket entering the crematorium furnace and them playing "Jesu, Joy of Man's Desiring," one of his favorite Bach compositions. I do not recall crying. I may have done. However, my grief has grown as I have become older. Due to losing my father at such a young age, I am much more aware of my role in the lives of my five children. Christmas, however, always has more than a trace of sadness.

Dad never thought I wanted to play music for a job. He had little or no interest in music in general, particularly music produced in the 1960s. My only musical memory of Dad is his singing "Hi-diddle-dee-dee, an actor's life for me..." when he let go of my bicycle saddle for the first time when I was a child. I pedaled on, oblivious that I was flying solo. I am twenty-one. My adult life—professional life—has begun, but my father has died.

Everything feels subdued and flattened. I find myself thinking about something that will occupy me at various times and in various shades for years to come: did Dad, in the end, believe his son made the correct decision? Was he impressed that I was finally making a living, although through an unconventional means? Was Grev Collins pleased as a father that his youngest had made it across the Atlantic?

I'd like to think he'd be proud in the end, but I've often wondered what the tipping point would have been. Perhaps filling four nights at Wembley? Or as another example: "My son, playing for the Prince of Wales—marvelous." The royal seal of approval would have granted the paternal seal of approval. That would have clinched it.

Postscript: During the drafting of this book, I noticed that Dad never had a marker set where his ashes were interred. I pledged to solve it, and Clive inquired. My brother discovered that Dad's ashes were never picked up due to a communication breakdown between him and Mum. As a result, Dad's earthly remains were left in the Southend Crematorium. No one knows where he is now.

Chapter 7: Lamb Lies Down, Singer Flies Off

Fortunately, I don't have much time to linger on my father's passing. The Foxtrot tour resumes in Croydon, south London, on January 7, 1973, six days after his funeral. It continues around the rest of Europe, back to the United Kingdom, and finally moves to North America, where we perform at Carnegie Hall. We won't be done until we reach Paris and Brussels on May 7 and 8. A tough spell of touring to deal with at a difficult period, with Peter's clothes becoming increasingly bizarre as the tour progressed.

Following the publication of Genesis Live, we scarcely paused before assembling to a lovely but slightly deteriorating country house in Chessington, Surrey, to begin work on the next album. I don't remember how we got there, but the owners were a nice couple with three attractive daughters. We put up our gear in their living room, so I'm assuming the couple was not around.

In the studio, the song did not strike us as particularly "pop," despite its pop-single duration. We had obtained a sitar-guitar, as used by The Beatles. Steve performed the fundamental riff, which sounded excellent, and I began to play a Beatles-esque rhythm, and things progressed from there. Peter's words were written fairly late since they were inspired by the Betty Swanwick picture (The Dream) on the album cover. My voice appears on the tune as part of a duet with Peter. And that's it. Genesis scores their first hit. We're heading to the Top of the Pops.

But we don't. We decline an offer from the BBC's weekly institution because we believe our audience will protest to our appearance on such a mainstream show. Fundamentally, we also oppose. We're carving our own route, and for the same reasons we don't trust festivals (we have no control over the staging, and it's not our audience), we don't trust television. Furthermore, we now take pride in our presentation skills, and "I Know What I Like" does not lend itself well to presentation. Not yet, anyhow. On tour with the album, Peter will wear a conical hat resembling a Boer War military helmet and, with some straw clamped between his teeth, imitate mowing a lawn with the drone that begins the song.

So, while we all love and trust him, we must be businesslike and consider our future. Especially when there are crippling bills to consider.

Tony Smith, on the other hand, is a partner in an established concert marketing company alongside Mike Alfandary and Harvey Goldsmith. Tony's father, John, was also a promoter—he promoted The Beatles and Frank Sinatra—and Tony had a top-tier apprenticeship with him. They also advertised the Charisma Package Tour. So Tony knows who to befriend or avoid, including prominent managers like Don Arden and Peter Grant. However, he decides to forego all of that guaranteed concert money to manage a band that is definitely on the rise—most notably, the bankruptcy court.

In the coming months, we become extremely popular on the East Coast. Almost deliriously popular. Having said that, we cannot take anything for granted. We have a terrible gig with The Spencer Davis Group at the poorly carpeted and acoustically dead Felt Forum beneath Madison Square Garden. We had hoped for something similar to the genuine Garden, but instead received its ugly cousin. Boston still appears to dislike us, but they'll come around someday.

In general, we play to puzzled looks across the United States, particularly in Ypsilanti, Evanston, Fort Wayne, and Toledo. In short, we're swimming against the musical flow. They had never heard of us. We're not as nerdy as Yes. We are not as virtuoso-driven as Emerson, Lake, and Palmer. We're far more eccentric than everyone else out there, and we pay the price.

By the time we get in Los Angeles, we're ready to relax. We stay at the Tropicana, a proper motel (which is exciting for us English boys). We move from room to room, spiffing up (this is LA!) and eating downstairs at Duke's coffee shop, a famous place where all the visiting bands congregate. LA is everything we expected it to be. All of the icons are visible, including the Whisky A Go Go, the Hollywood sign, and the Capitol Records Tower. Palm palms, warm weather, and the occasional tequila sunrise make us all very happy.

Tony Banks despises flying—he'll grow used to it later in life—and the rest of us aren't too keen either. We're not inspired with the idea of living the rock'n'roll ideal by touring the United States by bus. First, we are not rock and roll. We're not very interested in boozing and shagging on the team bus. "Clean sheets and cocoa," Mike Rutherford used to say whether the motel was to his liking. On a bus, I don't think any of us can sleep well wondering if someone is still awake behind the wheel of this coffin-shaped box full of bunks.

So there are two stretch limousines, each driven by a person named Joe.

Canadian customs are among the strictest. They're used to musicians coming over from America with a small supply of drugs. Bands have a tendency to forget that Canada is another country, which may have contributed to Keith Richards' iconic Toronto bust. Inevitably, as we enter Canada on our way to Toronto, Customs stops us at the Peace Bridge near the Niagara Falls border crossing. Our lighting technician, Les Adey, is a hardworking and eager toker as white as a sheet. Soon, our similarly white-as-a-sheet English bodies will be on show when we undergo a strip search. Regis Boff, our tour manager and reputed pillar of strength, is shaking like a leaf. Things do not look good.

Then they appear worse. As they begin rummaging through my belongings, I recall the small spliff-end I've been storing for a rainy day in my father's wallet, a memento mori that I now carry.

We carry on. Genesis plays Bill Graham's Winterland Ballroom in San Francisco—a legendary performance, but not for us. This is Jefferson Starship and Janis Joplin territory. They don't like limo-riding English beardies. The audience is clearly uninterested. But we have to travel to these locations since we don't receive much radio airplay. There are areas of DJ support—New York, Chicago, and Cleveland come to mind—but little else. This lack of reaction is, understandably, replicated in many of our shows. An eager crowd gathers in cities where we are broadcast. Where we battle for airplay, we struggle to attract an audience.

The South is hostile, a continental hinterland that Genesis cannot survive. They simply don't comprehend what we're about. We are the pinnacle, or the depths, of English foppishness. What exactly are they singing about? What are they playing? Is that makeup the singer is wearing? The only thing lacking in some locations is the chicken wire in front of the stage.

In New York, we perform three nights at the Academy of Music. But after our first gig, our instruments are stolen overnight. This seems like a significant infringement. Our important gear has vanished. We need to lie down. We even cancel the second event to facilitate our recovery and give Mike time to purchase new equipment. Can I borrow some? Are you mad? It would be like playing with another person's wife. We ultimately recuperate, perform the third show, and go on our way.

Back to UK, and the work continues. We play five nights in London's Theatre Royal Drury Lane, and Peter decides to go all out. After all, this is a theater, and they are used to flying Peter Pan around on cables. He put together a silver suit and a white painted face. When he removes his cape and fluorescent box head at the end of "Supper's Ready," he soars into the sky.

Within about four weeks following the end of that eight-month tour, in June 1974, we begin production on the album that will break us in every way. We're in Hampshire's Headley Grange, which was established in 1795 as a poorhouse but has since been used by Led Zeppelin and Bad Company for recording. Whichever band was there last has left it in a terrible, disgusting condition. Rats take advantage of this. They're everywhere, leaping up and down the creaky staircases, rustling up the creepers that cover the trees, and scrambling up the vines that surround the home. Dozens and hundreds of them. And that's all you can see. It is still a poor dwelling.

The only thing that redeems this place for me is that John Bonham recorded his great groove to "When the Levee Breaks" in the stairway.

I can almost smell it. Instead, I smell rats. There's thousands of them. I arrive last, with the best bedrooms already reserved, of course. So I have a filthy room filled with hot and cold running rats. At night, I can hear small feet scampering above and beneath me.

Because "Supper's Ready" performed so well on the Selling England tour, we decided to expand the concept of a tale song or suite of songs into a double album. Tommy, The Rise and Fall of Ziggy Stardust, and The Dark Side of the Moon were released during the age of concept albums. It doesn't seem intimidating or silly to us. Tommy stands out to me from the crowd. I'm a huge Who fan, and they had more magic than they knew what to do with.

Mike gets an unexpected idea to develop something based on the classic children's story The Little Prince, but it leads nowhere. More narrative ideas are being discussed. Peter and Tony must have gotten into a fight at some time, as Tony, in particular, does not want Peter to write all the words. But Peter's point is that if it's going to be a tale CD, only one person should write the story, and hence the album.

Things are awful at home—his wife, Jill, is having a tough pregnancy, something I was unaware of at the time. As a result, he is occasionally absent, leaving us to carry on without him. This makes it difficult to think as a team on such a large project.

From my perspective, Peter's departure does not have to be the end of the world. My stoutly practical solution is to reorganize Genesis into an instrumental quartet. At the very least, this allows the music to be properly heard.

The other three responded to this suggestion as follows: "Don't be that fucking foolish. Us, without singing or lyrics? "Get back into your box, Phil." Obviously, they are correct.

Before anything substantial can happen, Friedkin learns that his offer may cause the demise of Genesis. He does not desire that, especially since his sci-fi project is simply a vague concept. Several weeks after the offer is made, the plug is withdrawn.

So, Peter is back. But he's returned since a better deal didn't pan out. Circumstances are not ideal for a reunion. We keep working, forgive and forget, or at least pretend.

We then go in to record this collection of songs at Glaspant Manor, a Welsh farm, with Island Mobile Studios and John Burns. We discovered that the recording studio environment was suffocating us, and we were fighting to sound as energetic on record as we did live. Using John and a mobile studio, we make a move that provides some freedom. He's nearly beginning to feel like a member of the band.

Peter is still composing lyrics as the four of us record, but it's a relaxing respite, especially since it allows Peter, Mike, and Tony to indulge in their love of country walks. On tour, we'd frequently stop and get onions, carrots, cheese, and bread before heading to a field for a picnic. It sounds a little hippie, but there's nothing wrong with a good slice of Cheddar and an onion.

Back in London, we mixed The Lamb Lies Down on Broadway at Island Studios, Basing Street. After two months of recording our epic in Wales, we're thrilled to be back on home turf. While we're laying down the songs, we learn that Brian Eno is recording in the studio upstairs for his second solo album, Taking Tiger Mountain (By Strategy). I'm not a big fan of Roxy Music, but the other guys do. Peter comes up to say hello and asks if we may record some vocals using his computer. In exchange, Eno asks if I might go up and perform on one of his tracks, "Mother Whale Eyeless." I don't mind getting pimped out.

Eno and I hit it off. He's a fascinating character, not the typical "pop" person, which may be one of the reasons he departed Roxy Music, and I admire his working style. I end up performing on his albums Another Green World, Before and After Science, and Music for Films.

During the mixing sessions at Basing Street, a divide emerges between daytime Genesis and nighttime Genesis. Peter and I occasionally mix until two in the morning. Tony comes the next day, hates it, scrubs it. Sometimes we are still recording when we should be mixing. The time is short, the atmosphere is strained, and everyone is exhausted. There's too much music and lyrics, we're hurrying to complete, the narrative nuances of this double-vinyl concept album are a mystery to all of us (including, we suspect, Peter), and we're about to go on tour. A tour in which we have agreed to play the full record. A tour with a major production attached.

Inevitably, unavoidably, The Lamb Lies Down on Broadway promises the grand unveiling of a 23-track double album that no one has ever heard, played by a band who are themselves running to catch up, punting a concept on which the paint is still wet, tricked out with an ambitious production that has never been tested, on a world tour scheduled for 104 dates.

Despite Peter's approaching departure, most of my memories of the Lamb tour are positive. To be honest, I often feel like I'm in heaven. I'm wearing headphones to hear myself sing, and I have an excellent sound mix. Some of the pieces of music are particularly fun to play: "The Waiting Room" is fresh and different every night, and Tony's keyboard composition "Riding the Scree" and the quiet "Silent Sorrow in Empty Boats" are ambient pieces that are equally enjoyable.

However, the overall impression is of a band chasing their tails. The album was released in the United Kingdom on November 18, 1974, and the tour began in Chicago two days later, leaving even the most committed fans with little time to assimilate four sides of ambient-prog conceptualism. It's a huge amount to chew at one sitting at a show. Behind closed doors, things are getting a touch contentious at this far from auspicious start to any tour, let alone one of this scope, magnitude, and cost.

But bless the supporters; they do their best. By the end of the ninety-minute performance, with two versions of Peter onstage for the closing number "it." (a song with a lower-case, italics title and a full stop), everyone is seeing double. We prevail, but not in the sense we might have if the music and plot were more familiar.

The Lamb Lies Down Broadway tour will be mythologized, not least in This Is Spinal Tap. This trip would provide excellent fodder for screenwriters and actors. When does the pod not open? I've been there, stranded on stage with broken props and an unhappy guitarist. Is it any coincidence that Derek Smalls, Spinal Tap's bassist, resembles Steve Hackett at this point?

We occasionally play in front of half-full houses. Peter has his own dressing area in the back, complete with makeup and a mirror, and the four of us are free to visit. He's not a prima donna, but a lot of record business guys come into the dressing room afterward, shouting and puffing, "Great show, Pete!"

Their blowing dry ice up his arse bothers Tony and myself as well. Peter is recognized as a wonderful architect. Genesis is in risk of being eclipsed by him. Having said that, I don't recall Peter ever accepting the bait of stardom. Despite having his own dressing room, he felt like one of us backstage.

Finally, France, and the tour comes to a conclusion, much to everyone's satisfaction. Just before we go onstage in Besançon, a little, unassuming town on the Swiss border, Tony Smith informs us that the previous gig, in Toulouse, has been canceled due to a lack of interest. This appears to sum it up. So the penultimate show, at Besançon, becomes the final show. It dawns on us that this may be our final performance of "The Colony of Slippermen" and "Here Comes the Supernatural Anaesthetist." This is our final gig with Peter. This is the final time we'll see him crawling through a large cock. It's May 22, 1975.

We all agree to stay quiet about Peter's leaving for as long as feasible. We want to be ready with new material before word spreads.

And The Lamb Lies Down on Broadway now? It's one of the few Genesis albums I can put on and be startled by, and I don't recall ever listening to it in its full. But it's a high point for the band in certain ways, and the Spinal Tap reference is a praise, backhanded or not. To quote Peter's last words onstage with Genesis: "It's only rock'n'roll, but I like it."

As for me, I'm looking forward to seeing what tomorrow brings. After all, I now have additional, personal commitments. On the Canadian leg of the Selling England by the Pound tour, I reconnected with an old flame and was happy to learn she had a plus-one: an infant daughter.

We are halfway through the seventies. The decade began with me discovering a band, proceeded with my father's death, and now, in the middle, has me recast as a family man.

Chapter 8: Family Man, Frontman

Pause, rewind, and reflect.

It's March 1974, fourteen months until Peter departs Genesis. The Selling England by the Pound tour comes to Vancouver for a gig at the Garden Auditorium. I'm twenty-three, and I'm excited: Andrea Bertorelli, my on/off/on teenage sweetheart, now lives in this city on Canada's remote Pacific coast.

In the late 1960s, as Andy and I parted ways—as usual, since I reconnected with Lavinia Lang—so did our extended family links. Following Andy's father's death, her mother reestablished a friendship with a Canadian air force officer stationed in wartime Godalming, Surrey, married him, and moved to Vancouver. Andy, her sister Francesca, a Playboy bunny, and her brother John accompanied her.

By spring 1974, I hadn't seen Andy in three or four years. I do know some of her news, however. Mrs. Bertorelli writes to my mother, who recounts that Andy went into the bush, found someone, lived in a cabin for a short time, became pregnant, and was subsequently abandoned by the father. Andy returned to the family home in Vancouver and gave birth to a daughter called Joely Meri Bertorelli on August 8, 1972, two years to the day I joined Genesis.

Before the band arrives in Vancouver, I call to invite the Bertorelli family to the show. Andy's mother, always welcoming, requests that I stay with them during my brief visit to the city. It is a fantastic reunion. I eagerly accept Mrs. B.'s invitation to eat with her family. I meet Joe, the Canadian stepfather who enjoys tenpin bowling (I would support his team many years later), and sixteen-month-old Joely, a little peach. We hadn't even eaten dinner when Andy and I's old feelings flared again.

She's a gorgeous young lady with a beautiful figure. She's incredibly sexy, which is why she was so effective at crushing hearts. I have to admit that many of the lyrics to Genesis' 1986 song "Invisible Touch" were written about her.

Andy is pleased, as do I and Mrs. B., who has long wanted me as a son-in-law. By the time Genesis leaves Vancouver, Andy and I are back together. And I suppose I'm a father. Life has altered dramatically, yet I do not look back or sideways. Andy holds a bit of my heart from school. Does she have a daughter? I do not think twice about it.

This is hardly the ideal setting for partners, to say the least. As Peter will discover with his (literally) embryonic family, compassionate leave and family time do not exist in Genesis. We work evenings, weekends, and some or all of the Sabbaths. Then, as is customary, we pick up our tools and continue working. That's how it is.

Unfortunately, recording The Lamb coincides with touring The Lamb, making life in Genesis even more hectic than usual. Given the turmoil and the cost of the show, Andy and Joely are unable to accompany me on tour as frequently as we would like. From the beginning of our relationship, she has been compelled to be alone. She's been a rock'n'roll widow since day one. However, I don't recall this affecting Mike, Tony, or their partners; they appear to be everywhere. Perhaps I wasn't assertive enough.

I am aware that we encounter a variety of situations. Tapes by the bucket load. Guys singing along with our records. Playing guitar to our songs. Some men play piano, this and that. Some individuals email recordings of themselves singing over Frank Sinatra or Pink Floyd. We reduce them to a decent group before beginning auditions.

All relevant news and available facts contribute to the conclusion that Genesis is no longer a viable business. Steve's album was released just before this, in October 1975, before we had even begun recording A Trick of the Tail. Also not helping matters is the fact that I chose this time to begin seeing another band.

My on/off relationship with Brand X began in late 1974, when I received a call from Richard Williams. The former Melody Maker writer is currently the head of A&R at Island Records. He tells me he has an unusual group, a jam band he recently signed, and they're seeking for a new drummer.

I join them for rehearsals, and we have some fun. At the time, Brand X were more funk than jazz. They have a singer, but he often has nothing to do, so he hops on the congas. There's a lot of improvising with a groove and a single chord. Hours of it.

Nonetheless, I like these folks and the flexibility they provide, so I agree to work part-time for Brand X, although I have no idea what I'm getting into. There are no gigs and only vague whispers about an LP. However, the guitarist and singer soon depart to pursue other interests, leaving only bassist Percy Jones, pianist Robin Lumley, guitarist John Goodsall, and me.

When the four of us instrumentalists start performing, Brand X transforms into something completely different. These are the days of fusion and jazz-rock, some of which are far too noodly and self-indulgent for my tastes. However, we will release a few interesting records, particularly the first two, Unorthodox Behaviour (1976) and Moroccan Roll (1977).

But right now, in the autumn of 1975, the members of the Peter-less Genesis are all-for-one and one-for-all together. Our stubborn instinct is that we will show them. Was it all Peter? Did he write everything? Just because the fox's head is gone does not mean we are. We might need to locate a singer, but the new material he'll have to deal with is fantastic. Genesis' death rumors have been greatly exaggerated.

We're not just looking for someone with good vocals. Will he be a good writer? What will he contribute to the band? We're attempting to figure out if we want this individual in our family. Because Genesis, with our backs against the wall, is currently incredibly tight. A band of brothers.

I start to like these Monday routines, especially the opportunity to sing. It's long been assumed that on this album I might front a couple of the acoustic tracks, like "Entangled" or "Ripples." But I know I'll never be able to pull off "Squonk," "Dance on a Volcano," or any of the heavier songs.

It's a bit of an irony that it takes nearly 10 years for their songwriting skills to "mature" and produce big singles, which coincides with another rising reality: I'm becoming the singer-by-default, at least in the basement of Churchfield Road.

Every night, I go home to Andy.

"Find a singer yet?"

"No. "No one meets the requirements."

We auditioned five to six weeks. We've seen around thirty males. It's starting to get tedious. With the clock ticking—unsurprisingly, there's already discussion of another tour—we have no choice but to dedicate studio time. At the very least, we've written some strong material.

We enter Trident with a new co-producer, Dave Hentschel, and record at a rapid speed. I'm particularly interested with "Los Endos," which I based on the groove of Santana's "Promise of a Fisherman," from his recently released jazz-fusion album Borboletta. "Squonk" is quite Zeppelin-like. There's also "Robbery, Assault, and Battery," which demonstrates that Genesis' "story" songs still have a place.

We're quite delighted with these songs. They have a loud, fresh, and unique sound. We feel and sound like a new band.

Deep down, I know I can do it, but singing it is a very different story. Sometimes your intellect says yes, but your voice shouts nay.

But I have a go, even if Mike's lyrics keep me guessing. Mike and Tony subsequently told me it was like a cartoon lightbulb moment. They stare at each other in the control room, and their brows say it all: By George, I believe he has it! Looking back, that was a watershed event for me. The studio environment was ideal, allowing us to work tirelessly until the vocals and music came together. I still didn't want to go out and sing.

And yet... We are still bewildered and puzzled. The hoped-for vocalist has failed to deliver. The drummer's pop doesn't sound horrible. But over the entire album? Is this wise?

Certain songs are very demanding. "Mad Man Moon" is one of Tony's compositions, and his melodies are outside of my regular comfort zone, especially when you have to learn them on the fly in the studio. I'd get used to it over the next few years. "A Trick of the Tail" is also his, but it sounds more natural to me. Overall, singing the record was easier than I expected.

I'm coming around to this viewpoint, albeit tentatively and grudgingly, with certain caveats and slightly gritted teeth. Finally, I am the agent of my own death.

Bill fits in well, although he is the type of drummer who enjoys playing something new every night. Although I understand his desire to keep things fresh, some drum fills are cues, which Tony, Mike, and Steve rely on.

Then we have lift-off. Another tour and another chapter.

A Trick of the Tail debuts in February 1976. This new Genesis team is obviously feeling the underdog. Perhaps this is one of the reasons it has received favorable reviews: expectations for the band's future viability have been quite low. Then people hear the song and think it's fantastic, and these underdogs may have had their last bark: the album hits number three in the UK charts, which, reassuringly, matches the achievement of Selling England by the Pound.

The following month, we traveled to Dallas for live rehearsals. The Trick of the Tail tour kicks out on March 26 in London, Ontario, Canada. I'm not really nervous about singing or performing in front of an audience. I was used to that on Oliver! a long time ago. However, the challenge is performing with only a microphone stand between myself and the crowd, rather than a row of cymbals. If you're not like bat-wing headgear and flying through the air, what do you do when there's no singing?

There are other practical considerations. I've previously stated unequivocally that I will be unable to replicate Peter's success. I will not be wearing Andy's camisole or badger pelt. But what shall I wear? The workman's overalls that accomplished the job when I was only the drummer? Is that too workmanlike? I can put on a flat cap and an Edwardian coat for "Robbery, Assault, and Battery," but that's about as dramatic as I'm willing to get.

It was suggested that I get some garments made. These will be completed in time for the opening event, but I'm not going to make my debut as a singer wearing something other than myself. I need to feel completely at ease. Worker's overalls it is.

The lights go out at the London Arena. I curse softly and gulp noisily. What will this be like? Everyone is afraid. I've taken my responsibilities seriously, so there's no quick, confidence-boosting drink or spliff. Suddenly, the magnitude of this situation strikes me. Genesis will play a new singer. Most bands would not even take that chance, let alone survive it. Many have thought we won't, and have already written our epitaph: "Genesis: in the beginning was the word..." It ended up being a nightmare when they attempted to replace a talented singer with an adept drummer. "May they rest in pieces."

I spend virtually the whole show cowering behind the microphone stand; I'm a twenty-four-year-old, drumstick-thin slip of a person. And I do not even touch the microphone. Removing it from its current position would be excessive. singer-y. But I make it through the show with only minor wounds and bruises to my delicate confidence as a frontman.

Aside from the wardrobe incident, the first two shows go extremely well. We do The Lamb Medley—let's give the audience something familiar—but none of the material is intimidating. Everything is quite familiar to me. I've heard that several times. And it is up to us to play the fan favorites, no matter how difficult, epic, or heavy. We must convey the important message as clearly as possible: Genesis continues with its normal operations.

Even so, when I'm singing, my hands remain firmly in my pockets for extended periods of time. It will be some time before I touch the microphone, remove it from its holder, and start walking around with it. Only when that happens do I believe it is official: I, Phil Collins, am a singer.

It's a six-week tour of the United States, marking the first stage of a globe tour. America is still our top focus. We get blank eyes in Germany—they didn't like us until Duke in 1980—but we know we can make money in the States.

Led Zeppelin are ahead of us, having already ascended the peak. Our British colleagues include Yes, Emerson, Lake & Palmer and Supertramp. However, we still haven't had an international smash single. We are still only being played on FM radio. We are a cult band. A big cult band.

I draw strength from the reviews and interviews, and Andy's encouragement when she and Joely visit me on tour. Everyone is shocked by how delicious it is. "Wow," they tell me. "You sound terrific. It sounds like Peter." I'm not sure that's a compliment. But at this point, I'll accept anything.

The positive reactions keep flowing. Genesis and our fans exhale jointly beginning in London, Ontario. We're relieved to learn that our de facto solution to the problem of Peter's departure worked better than we could have imagined. Replacing Peter from outside would have been extremely difficult. Arguably, replacing him from inside is just as difficult.

We return home in May, and after a month off, I make my British debut as Genesis' singer on June 9, 1976, at the Hammersmith Odeon for the first of six nights.

On the one hand, I'm somewhat settled as a vocalist. On the other hand, after a lengthy run of concerts in the United States, you become accustomed to the rowdy audience response. The Americans' ambient noise during the show is surprisingly loud. When the band returns to Europe, they are met with reverent silence: "Fuck, they're listening." Everybody tightens their belts.

The tour concludes in the summer of 1976, and by September, we're at Relight Studios in Hilvarenbeek, the Netherlands, recording Genesis' eighth album, Wind & Wuthering, with the indispensable Dave Hentschel producing. This is our first time recording abroad of the United Kingdom. We completed all the backing recordings in twelve days. Our momentum feels doubled.

However, the most significant thing in my life right now is that Andy is about to give birth to our first child together. This would be significant even at the best of times, but having been so far away for so long adds emotional resonance. Andy has been pregnant since the beginning of 1976, thus she was unable to join me on much of the Trick of the Tail tour. While she has been stuck at home in Ealing, I have been out in the world, attempting to become a frontman.

Simon Philip Nando Collins was born September 14, 1976. Philip followed me, and Nando followed Andy's father. In principle, Genesis might have postponed the album's release so that I could be home for the birth without fear or emergency sprints back across the North Sea. But it's Genesis, and the show must go on. In retrospect, I could have said, "Fuck Genesis, I'm off to look after my wife." But we're all supposed to give our all to the band, even if there are later repeated attempts to reverse-engineer such situations: "Well, if only you'd told us, we could have moved the start-date." However, while becoming the frontman has given me confidence as a performer, I am too shy to speak up in private. Old social hierarchies, domestic or professional, persist.

Bill Bruford left after the Trick of the Tail tour to establish his own band, U.K., therefore the band is once again in flux. I refer to the legendary American drummer as Chester Thompson. I've seen him with Weather Report and heard him on Frank Zappa's live CD Roxy and Elsewhere, where he was joined by Ralph Humphrey, a second drummer. They play a wonderful double drum riff in Zappa's song "More Trouble Every Day"—I want it in our band.

I phone Chester, and despite having never met us, he says yes. We do some rehearsals, and he's in. Chester will be with us until the conclusion of our reunion tour in 2007.

The months fly by. On July 3, 1977, we completed the Wind & Wuthering tour at Munich's Olympiahalle, took the month of August off, and began work on our ninth album in September. That month, Simon is one.

The Genesis fan base is growing rapidly and consistently. We're currently playing big arenas, and things couldn't be going better professionally. However, my absence is having a negative impact on my family life. Andy, who has two small children, is housebound and frustrated.

During this period, Steve's frustration has become clear. He launched his solo record, but instead of relieving the pressure, it worsened it. He wants to include more songs on Genesis albums. One man's meat is another man's poison: Genesis' new configuration has unexpectedly opened up new songwriting opportunities, and while I'm feeling more secure as a writer, Steve is still not getting the creative space he believes he deserves.

That summer, we're in London mixing Seconds Out, a live album recorded during our four-night residency at Paris' Palais des Sports in June. I'm driving from Queen Anne's Grove to Trident when I spot Steve on the street in Notting Hill.

So Steve goes and another dies. However, if we can endure the loss of a singer, we can also survive the loss of a guitarist. We continue on, undeterred, with Mike working hard on bass and lead.

In the autumn, we returned to Hilvarenbeek to record another album, which was completed by the end of the year. And then there were three. Genesis has never been so successful. The threesome is working, and my singer role is working. There is a sensation that we are going to reach a new level. If only we're willing to put forth the effort. Yes, even more legwork than we've done already.

What about the house fires? They are both fading down and flaring up. Andy has spent a lot of time alone as a mother of two young children. When I am home for an extended period of time, the environment is tight. We can only say a few sentences before we start bickering. We love each other, to be sure, but there are times when we clearly dislike each other.

In a relationship, each partner must complement the other. This is not happening in our marriage. I'm not the type of person who harbors suspicions or, dare I say, paranoia. Andy, on the other hand, notices an odd expression or something someone says and examines it closely, endlessly, and exhaustingly. I'm having difficulty dealing with this, therefore the drawbridge is raised.

In fact, neither is doing well. I'm being dragged this way and that. I've progressed from drummer to rock star, but at my core, I'm still a family man and father. I stare into Simon's cot and think, "You have no idea what's happening." I don't think I do either. I want my sons and daughters to have a father and a normal family life. However, the current situation suggests we will all be disappointed. Genesis's success is against us.

It's been less than four years since my teenage lover and I reconnected in Vancouver. In that period, we've experienced seismic shifts such as a transatlantic relocation, the establishment of a family, the departure of a frontman, the promotion of a drummer, and the metamorphosis of a student-favorite cult band into an international rock sensation. My role as a Genesis singer has boosted my career in ways I never expected. However, it appears that it is also hastening the end of my personal life.

But do I have any regrets or resentments about the band or what it has done to me? I cannot say I do. There was no alternative. I needed to take over.

Chapter 9: The Divorce That Roared

In early 1978, as our new album title suggests, And then there were three.

Tony Banks, Mike Rutherford, and I had just finished recording when Tony Smith called a band meeting. These are regularly held to debate our future and typically include us assembling at the band's headquarters in London, moaning and drinking tea.

Genesis gatherings are always a great place for debate. Smith suggests something, and I say, "How many times do I have to tell you, I don't want to fucking do..." Insert the name of the tour, promotional commitment, or Top of the Pops performance. And, according to your timetable, a month is four weeks, not five, therefore we won't be able to do all of that job." And then I give in.

Of course, no consideration is given to the potential that America will shatter us. Or, more particularly, break one of us and his marriage.

Smith and our long-term agent, Mike Farrell, schedule a rigorous American tour. Then another. Then another. Then there were three American tours in rapid succession. Plus, there are two European tours. Finally, there will be a brief visit of Japan.

I say, "OK," and give in again.

I go home and report to Andrew. "Darling, great news—Genesis have a fantastic chance to make some serious inroads in America..." To me, the professional reasoning of touring our arses for the better part of a year is flawless. Emotional, personal or marriage logic? Let's say I'm not entirely clear on that front.

Andy and I recently purchased Old Croft in Shalford, near Guildford, Surrey, which is a little further from London than we had planned. It's almost as nice as Peter's parents' house, located along winding country roads. I've moved from the end of the line to the end of the lane. However, I am not affluent at the moment. A Trick of the Tail, released two years prior, was the record on which Genesis began to credit the writers individually, resulting in individual royalties. Despite the success of "And Then There Were Three," my songwriting income remains low. Now we have a large mortgage and a young, growing family—Simon is one and a half and Joely is five.

Another reason I'm doing all of this touring is less apparent, and it stems from my childhood. Despite avoiding the unpleasant prospect of working in the City, I am still my father's son. I'm the breadwinner and provider for my family, so I need to go out and work. Do not buy a guitar-shaped swimming pool or a champagne-colored Rolls-Royce. Because, quite simply, it is my responsibility. I return home knowing I have to deal with this awful turn of events, but also knowing that I have to leave on another tour almost shortly. And touring in the 1970s is not the same as touring today. There are no emails, Skype, FaceTime, or cell phones. We're not too far from the telegram days.

As a result, when I get home, we have a lot to talk about. However, when we attempt to communicate, we get nowhere. I realize this isn't Andy's perspective, but this is exactly how I recall it.

Andy called me at home one afternoon when I was with the kids and said, "I'm not coming home tonight. "I'm staying out." And I know who I am.

There's all this loose coin in a small tray beside the phone, and before I lash out at another wall, I throw it across the hall. I have no intention of becoming physically violent, yet this is the closest I've come.

This will undoubtedly have an impact on the children. Later, I hear Joely and Simon playing mother and father in the dining room. Simon enters with his pedal car. Joely asks, "What are you doing back?" "You are not supposed to be here!" From the mouths of babies.

When we arrive in Japan for the final leg, it's not just the plates spinning. As Mike Rutherford will later describe in his book, The Living Years, I am legless in Japan after discovering sake, but I am never unable to perform. I also understand the mind-numbing nature of being so far ahead of GMT. For the average European, Japan forty years ago was like being in a completely alien country, without knowing or understanding anything; blind to language, customs, and norms; and dealing with a time difference that made it nearly impossible to contact anyone back home. It's completely disorientating. So I clutch to sake in a nightmare haze.

When I returned to the United Kingdom at the end of 1978, my most vivid memory was of a café in the village of Bramley, Surrey, not far from Old Croft. It's strange what you remember during a time of difficulty. I recall ordering risotto. I recall being unable to eat it. Andy also told me it was the end of our relationship. Not only that, but she's taking our kids and returning to Canada.

Andy departs for Vancouver during the not-so-festive season, so I'm dreaming of a grey Christmas. But I'm not going to give up my marriage without another fight. I instruct some of the Genesis road crew to pack up the Old Croft furniture because, in early 1979, I decide to accompany her there. I plan to reside in Vancouver, buy a house, and win my wife back.

By April 1979, I'm back in Shalford, tail between my knees, boxes still stacked in the house where I'd scarcely lived. The paint is still almost completely wet on the walls. The paint was done by the guy who has been sleeping with my wife. We went with wooden floorboards and a brick interior—very late-seventies chic—making it look even more lonely. Everything, including myself, has been stripped to its essence. I am rattling around in this place, just me and the cardboard boxes. I would have returned to Genesis right away, but Mike and Tony have taken advantage of my emotional hiatus to start working on the solo albums they've long desired. During 1979, both spent time in Stockholm recording at ABBA's Polar Studios. They had not anticipated that my visit to Vancouver would be so brief. Neither had I.

To avoid entirely losing control, I begin diverting my energies into whatever musical distraction I can find. Someone refers me to English singer-songwriter John Martyn, who produced the iconic 1973 folk jazz album Solid Air. John asks me to drum on the record that will be called Grace & Danger. As we get closer, he realizes I can sing, and I provide background vocals on the lovely "Sweet Little Mystery."

Throughout these sessions, I fell in love with John and his music. He and I seem to have a musical connection—so much so that two years later, I produce his next album, Glorious Fool. But before that, Grace & Danger is perhaps one of his best works. Unfortunately, Chris Blackwell, the head of Island Records, is not so confident. John, like myself, is going through a divorce, which is perhaps one of the reasons we have such a close relationship. But Blackwell believes the songs are too close. John and his wife Beverley collaborated on Island records, and Blackwell is extremely close to both. As a result, he's hesitant to share such an emotionally charged collection of music.

During this time, John frequently visits and plays at my house, and we alternate calling our soon-to-be ex-partners. It always ends with shouting and the phone going down.

We open another bottle.

So it goes on.

Given the historical interest in the purported friction between Gabriel-era Genesis and Collins-era Genesis, it's surprising that I'm playing with Peter so much right now. If I may be so bold, I am the best drummer he knows. He can depend on me. Peter, as a drummer, is quite choosy.

Later in 1979, we reconvene at London's Townhouse Studios, where I play drums on four tracks on his third solo album, produced by Steve Lilywhite and mixed by Hugh Padgham. Notably, I play on "Intruder," the song on which we created the so-called "gated" drum sound. More on that later.

Meanwhile, for moral support, two Brand X members, Peter Robinson and Robin Lumley, relocate to Old Croft. In retrospect, this was not a terribly sensible decision. They are much bigger party animals than I am.

Robin comes his American girlfriend Vanessa, and she and I begin a relationship. (Robin is quite pleased with it. He's a little bored with her. We are very late-seventies elegant, remember.) Peter lives at one end of the home, while Robin lives at the other, in what would have been one of the children's bedrooms. I enter what would have been the master bedroom. Alone. The marital suite never felt less romantic.

Before our first brief American tour, Brand X records an album, Product, at Tittenhurst Park in Berkshire. This is the John Lennon pad from the "Imagine" video, which he later "gave" to Ringo Starr. Although it remains Ringo's, it now functions as a studio, and when Brand X is in residence, it operates 24 hours a day. Brand X exists both day and night. I'm on the dayshift.

I also began spending my lunches and evenings at the Queen Victoria bar in Shalford. Nick and Leslie Maskrey, my landlord and landlady, become excellent friends and confidants who support me through difficult times. I will spend many sessions there, some with Eric Clapton. He's a country neighbor in Surrey, but I met him earlier that year when I was in the studio with John Martyn in London.

In these post-Andy dog days of '79, free of Genesis distractions, I visit Hurtwood Edge almost every day, frequently staying late. I befriend all of Eric's Ripley friends, whom he has known since he was a teenager. We frequently fly together to London to watch football games at Tottenham and West Ham, though Eric is a devoted West Brom fan.

Eric is too drunk to drive one Sunday after a heavy session at his Ripley local pub. I've gone with him in one of his finest Ferraris, and we need to get it home. He takes the passenger seat, while I take the driver's. I have never driven a Ferrari. Eric says he'll change gears, and all I have to do is use the clutch, brake, and accelerator while steering. This would be a struggle even if I wasn't the guy who couldn't drive the Hillman Imp or Mini Traveller in Genesis. It's mayhem, and I'm beginning to feel terrible for the Ferrari's precision-engineered gearbox. But somehow we make it to his place, and both the automobile and I exhale.

Sometimes we play pool into the early hours, drinking and laughing, then laughing and drinking some more. We have blues nights at The Queen Victoria after my blue days. It's the beginning of a wonderful friendship, and a short-term lifesaver for me, and Eric and I will continue to play important roles in each other's lives, both personally and professionally, for many years.

In a way, I relish the unexpected, undesired independence. I've never really just "hung out" with other musicians. Until now, my career has consisted of my joining a lineup; I've never formed a band with a group of friends. This partying with friends is new to me, and I'm loving it.

Brand X does it both on record (Robin is credited with "gunfire and chainsaw") and on stage, when the boys play jazz cowboys and Indians. We perform slightly mad Python-style shows with bleating sheep and barking dog sound effects. Brand X does a wonderful job of rescuing me from myself, for a while.

But these high jinks, as amusing and necessary as they are, must eventually come to a stop. I enjoy working and making music too much. So I stop their partying, and the boys leave. I started writing, but I'm not sure what I'm writing. Not yet. One of our long-time staff members, tech/studio wizard Geoff Callingham, investigates the best home-recording equipment, and we all purchase one. And suddenly, I want one of those CR-78s. I decide that the master bedroom, which would have been my marriage bedroom, will be my studio. That seems like an appropriate shift of use.

I relocate my great-aunt Daisy's 1820 vintage, straight-stringed Collard & Collard piano up there. I also own a Fender Rhodes piano and a Prophet-5 synthesizer. Fortunately, the previous owner of Old Croft was an old naval chap, a captain of some size. I run into him at The Queen Victoria one night (he's simply moved down the lane), and he mentions that he had the joists strengthened upstairs. For him, it was about accommodating his large bath; for me, it's about bearing the weight of Daisy's piano and my future, whatever it may be.

In my impromptu studio in my empty, echoing, house-is-not-a-home gaff in leafy Surrey, I'm just playing in every sense of the word. Tinkering. My ambitions are low. My technological understanding ends right before I open the instruction manual. I'm pleased when I watch the desk meters move and hear something play back. It means I actually recorded stuff. At this point, it doesn't matter what.

I program some rudimentary drum machine components and play around on the eight-track. Come back from the pub at lunchtime—after two pints of bitter, at most—and mess about some more. My doodles have gradually taken shape over the course of a year. But these are doodles. Nothing is truly prepared or done.

Nonetheless, without my even realizing, doodles evolve into sketches, outlines, and mini-portraits. Become tunes.

What are the words? They just come out of me without warning. This is true information. This is like jazz. When recording the guiding vocal, I improvise the words. Sounds move about in my lips, becoming syllables, words, phrases, and sentences.

One day, out of nowhere, I come up with a great chord progression. It's at the opposite extreme of the scale as "The Battle of Epping Forest." As I feel my way about my new studio and experiment with the sounds that are emerging in my head, recollections of early Genesis songs like that, as well as those on The Lamb, bleat through my head—music that was composed with no notion what would go on top, so it was all a little hectic.

This still-tentative tune exemplifies where I'm "at" as a relatively inexperienced songwriter. What is it about? I have no notion because, with the exception of perhaps one or two lines or sentences, it is entirely improvised. I still have the sheet of paper with the original scribbles, with the decorator's letterhead—not that one, but the original one, Robin Martin, who hired the undercoating cuckolder—at the top. I would record what I had just sung.

"In the Air Tonight" is 99.9 percent spontaneously performed, with the lyrics coming out of nowhere.

"If you told me you were drowning, I would not lend a hand": I know this is motivated by hatred and aggravation. That is what was happening. "Wipe off that grin, I know where you've been, it's all been a pack of lies": I'm shooting back, refusing to take it lying down, giving it everything I have.

This is a message for Andrew. When I call to speak with her in Vancouver, I have trouble getting through, physically and figuratively. I don't appear to be reaching her.

So I communicate through singing. When Andy hears these words, she will understand how much wounded I am, how much I love her, and how much I miss my children. Then it will be OK.

There's more where it came from: "Please Don't Ask" and "Against All Odds" were also penned around this period.

Then again, I just informed her that if she drowned, I wouldn't help. These are up and down periods. What I write is based on the phone talks we've just had, or attempted to have.

There is no discernible structure to the song sketches I gradually gather during 1979, and the idea that I'm Making My First Solo Album remains nebulous and remote. Feelings and intentions change daily. One day, Andy might irritate me by repeatedly slamming the phone down. Then, that night in the home studio, I'd be full of "fuck you" vibes. But the next day, I may write something like "You Know What I Mean." Something more mournful, emotional, shattered, and bereaved.

From raw emotion arises natural truth. The lyrics and message of "In the Air Tonight," I later realized, are far more than the sum of their parts. "I've been waiting for this moment all my life, oh Lord…" This is entirely subliminal and subconscious. Those words complemented the music. The verses have a storyline, but there is no direct link to the fury. And those words have been examined numerous times. Some guy handed me a thesis he'd completed for his college degree; he'd counted how many times I used the word "the." Others propose conspiracy ideas concerning an apparent drowning that I once witnessed.

What does "In the Air Tonight" mean? It indicates I'm moving forward with my life, or trying to.

Chapter 10: Ace Value

What do Tony and Mike think of my DIY scribblings? Do I give them the choice of utilizing "In the Air Tonight" on the Genesis album that will become 1980's Duke? Do I, in a nutshell, display my solitary hand?

The jury is still out. My 1979 batch of writing is complete. These songs are by no means professionally recorded, but the demos are complete. And, after a year of each of us recording on our own, Mike and Tony have completed their first solo projects, Smallcreep's Day and A Curious Feeling, and are eager to begin the next collective project. Which is great with me—at this point, I'm not thinking of this collection of infant pieces as a "album." But one thing is certain: these are the most intimate songs I've ever written, born out of the emotional wreckage of my failed marriage. As a result, by the time we start working on Duke as the 1970s come to an end, I'm a little protective about these tunes.

I propose transferring the writing sessions for the upcoming Genesis record to the second master bedroom at Old Croft, which Tony and Mike readily accept. In terms of band music, closets are empty. Except for a few tracks, Mike and Tony have exhausted their best material on their individual albums. Nonetheless, Genesis has thrived during their solo-album time. Big relief, big release of pressure. Previously, when Tony came in with an already finished composition, he'd kind of push it through: "This is a song I wrote, so this is what I want Genesis to do." It wasn't spoken explicitly, but it was implied.

In late 1979, we relocated from Old Croft to Stockholm's Polar Studios. The material we've created for Duke is excellent, and I'm still very much on the learning curve as a songwriter. I only started writing "properly" a year ago. However, other than the addition of "Misunderstanding" and "Please Don't Ask," my role in Genesis remains unchanged. Tony and Mike like these songs, but I believe I am still mostly known as the band's arranger. However, I am gradually gaining confidence and moving forward.

Mike has this sluggish guitar riff in an unusual time signature, 13/8, that I recommend speeding up. That becomes, "Turn It On Again." I use the CR-78 on "Duchess," which is the first time we've used that drum machine in studio. I've used it for demos, and after a year in my bedroom with it, I know what it can and cannot accomplish. It's extremely limited, but it works particularly well on "Duchess."

At one point, "Behind the Lines," "Duchess," "Guide Vocal," "Turn It On Again," "Duke's Travels," and "Duke's End" are loosely combined into a thirty-minute track about a figure named Albert. Lionel Koechlin, a French illustrator, created the album cover art. But we know a single piece that long will only be compared to "Supper's Ready," so we decide not to go there again. It's a new decade, and perhaps "suites" that take up an entire side of an album will no longer be as popular. A thorough clean-up is required.

By the time the record is released on March 28, 1980, we have already begun the Duke Tour. That day, in the middle of three nights at London's Hammersmith Odeon, Eric Clapton—who came at Pattie's suggestion—realizes I'm more than a pool-playing drinking buddy and Ferrari gearbox mangler. He recognizes me as a fellow musician, which I later learn surprises him. The tour travels around the United Kingdom until early May, then takes a week off before returning to Canada for a North American leg that will go until the end of June.

The third Canadian show is in Vancouver, and I use the occasion to call Andy. Although the divorce is still ongoing, I continue to hold a candle for her and miss my children deeply. I'm thinking, "This could be the time we fix things." The band spends about three days in town, and I stay with her mother. We have always been close, and I adore Mrs. B., with or without her child.

Back in the United Kingdom in the summer of 1980, I returned to the songs I had written the previous year. It's time to put my recordings where my heart is.

I hadn't planned on playing anything of mine to Ahmet. But I always kept a tape in my car so I could listen to the recordings and come up with new ideas to incorporate. Anyway, Ahmet listens to these demos and exclaims enthusiastically, "THIS IS A RECORD!" He suddenly forgets the new Genesis record. "Phil, you've got to turn this into a record. I will help you with anything I can. But this must be a record. Wow. This statement from this man, whom I greatly respect, is extremely essential. Ahmet discovered Aretha Franklin, Ray Charles, and Otis Redding, and now he tells me I, too, am a winner. He's made a number of records that I'm quite fond of, and he approves of my work. It does not get better than this.

And I need it. After my marriage ended, I felt humiliated. I had told the boys I was going to Vancouver to make things right, but I had returned empty-handed. Then Tony and Mike went on other individual musical experiences, leaving me as the singing drummer.

So, yeah, I've been feeling really horrible about myself. However, one of the greatest record executives in history tells me that what I've been doing on my own is fucking fantastic. Ahmet's approval finally convinces me that, once I finish my Duke duties, I will record my first solo album.

Still, I can't help but notice one final irony: if my marriage hadn't failed, my debut collection of solo songs might have turned out very differently. It would have most likely been Brand X style instrumental jazz, similar to Weather Report. If it wasn't so sad, it would be amusing.

I met Jill Tavelman in Los Angeles in mid-1980, following Genesis' performance at the Greek Theatre as part of the Duke tour. Tony Smith is also going through a divorce, so we're both newly single. Typically, management and I do not hang together after gigs, although we do occasionally go out together.

We sneak into a booth and sit down to satisfy our post-gig thirst. I extend my arms above and behind my head. Suddenly, a pair of hands grasp my hands. I look back and see this girl with short hair who is quite cute in a Tinkerbell sort of manner. She's extremely delighted. And she is with another female. Before long, we're all seated at the same table.

Eventually, the four of us board the waiting vehicle and head to L'Hermitage, the LA hotel of the moment. I'm still not sure how this happened, but later that night, I'm in bed with Jill and her girlfriend. That has not occurred before or subsequently. I should stress there is no hanky panky. My overriding thought is, "What am I supposed to do with two?" For others, this is their life. Not for me. I'm embarrassed, I suppose. For young(ish) Phil Collins, it's stage fright time.

Jill accepts my invitation to join me on tour and arrives in Atlanta five days later. Unfortunately, there is another Collins staying at the Hyatt Regency, so Jill is given the key to his room. He's a proper musician— a Scottish bagpipe player in town with his clan to perform in full Highland regalia—and when she walks into his room, he's in the shower. When he hears a feminine voice, he gets excited, believing it is in the fine print of his contract. By a whisker, normal modesty is retained, albeit Jill is brutally deprived of solving the enigma that perplexes most Americans: what a Scotsman wears beneath his kilt.

Suddenly, it seems we are an object. I respond in a way that is quickly becoming second nature to me: I write about her, with "This Must Be Love" and "Thunder and Lightning" emerging with love-filled ease. We converse on the phone daily, and then a few months later, when I return to LA to record horn parts for my upcoming solo album, Jill arrives to the studio. She brings her mother and introduces us. Afterward, her lovely mother Jane will respond, "Well, darling, love is blind." That burns a little, but I turn my pain into gain: the line will appear in the lyrics of a song, "Only You Know and I Know," from 1985's No Jacket Required.

Working with Eric is simple. He and Pattie's house in Ewhurst is only fifteen minutes from Shalford, so I frequently spend the night there. Pattie takes a genuine shine to me, and I've had a soft spot for her since I first saw her as a schoolgirl in A Hard Day's Night. So much so that Eric once joked to Mick Fleetwood at a New Year's Eve party that I'm fucking Pattie while he's out on the road—and also fucking Mick's ex-wife Jenny (Pattie's sister) in the process. Mick appreciates the joke, but I am embarrassed by the crack, especially since Joely and Simon are standing next to me.

So I'm always around there. We drink, and Eric occasionally needs to be sent to bed, but it never gets out of control. That's the type of person—or drinker—he is. He moves to the edge. I'm overly sensible. I'll leave the edge to others.

Even though I aim to make the most of my inexperience by producing these songs myself, I know I'll need an assistant producer and an engineer. So I met with Hugh Padgham. Hugh is a bassist, but he enjoys drums, and we created that breakthrough sound on Peter's single "Intruder." With hindsight, I realize that the day or two we spent working on Peter's third album at Townhouse in 1979 was life-changing.

I tell Hugh, "I can't stand recording all of this again. It was written with a lot of heart, and I appreciate how it sounds. So I'd like to use my demos. So we duplicate my eight-tracks onto sixteen-track, which was cutting-edge at the time, and continue to overdub at Townhouse over the winter of 1980/1981.

It's simple, ghostly, full of space, and a cri de coeur. It should absolutely not be a single.

I need to come up with an album title. It is evident that the majority of the songs are autobiographical. So I decided to call it Exposure. Or interiors. They sound fitting. But then I realize that Exposure isn't just a Robert Fripp record; it's also one on which I played. Interiors is a Woody Allen movie. I still loved that as a title. But, may labeling it Interiors make the painter and decorator believe it's all about him?

Because this is such a personal record, I am entirely dedicated to it, including all of the nuts and bolts. For starters, there's the question of which label will release it—and it won't be one associated with Genesis. Even if it meant disappointing our Charisma label owner and my old friend Tony Stratton-Smith, who, a chaotic decade ago, directed me to the Genesis gig in the first place.

I have a sad liquid meeting with him in his chamber at L'Hermitage to deliver the awful news. He's in Los Angeles because the Monty Python group is performing at the Hollywood Bowl, and John Cleese swings by to greet Strat. It's a very Fawlty moment, with him wearing a Pittsburgh Penguins hockey jersey. Sorry, I didn't realize you were busy. "Don't worry, come back later," Cleese says. The whiskey from our meeting does not go well with the tequila from our Mexican meal. I'll finish with a Strat cigar. I'm as ill as a Norwegian parrot on the pavement. Perhaps it's fitting atonement for abandoning my former patron.

Anyway, onward. Tony Smith sells Face Value across United Kingdom and Virgin is eager. I sign on the dotted line for Richard Branson's label, which includes Tubular Bells and Never Mind the Bollocks. I can fit someplace between those two. For the casual spectator, this is a new Phil Collins.

I travel to New York and meet with Ahmet to discuss how to promote this difficult-to-pin-down album. I've decided to stick with Atlantic for the US release, owing primarily to Ahmet. He adores me and my music and intends to keep that affection for the rest of his life. Over the years, he has given me a lot of strength and encouragement while I've been getting hit all over the place. When Ahmet has new musicians in his office, he will play "In the Air Tonight" and remark, "Now this is what I would like from you."

I invited Jill to move to England at the end of October 1980, and by 1981, we were settled in Old Croft. She gave up her senior year of college, where she was studying to be a high school teacher, to come live with me.

Face Value is released on February 9, 1981, just after my 30th birthday. I don't go on solo tours. It's too soon for any of that, and I'd like to expand my musical repertoire. Furthermore, the prospect of a solo tour is somewhat scary.

Meanwhile, Genesis has chosen to bite the bullet and establish our own studio/headquarters. We purchase a wonderful Tudor property in Chiddingfold, influenced in no small part by the enormous, multi-car garage in the garden. This can be converted into the recording space for the facility we'll call The Farm. While the building is being converted, we move into the house's low-ceilinged living room and began writing what would become Genesis' eleventh studio album, Abacab.

While writing Abacab, news of Face Value's unexpected success gradually spreads. This makes things rather tricky. I'll walk in all cheerful and really amazed: "My God, 'In the Air Tonight' has reached number 1 in Holland!" Not only that, but it's becoming a global success. Face Value continues to sell. As Tony Banks states succinctly in the 2014 BBC documentary Genesis: Together and Apart, "We wanted Phil to do well. "Just not very well."

In the early 1980s, I can already see how things would alter in the band. I assume the boys are thinking, "That's it—Phil's leaving." Not that anyone says so, but Tony Smith specifically tells me, "I think Genesis is really good for you." Is another Genesis singer leaving? Losing one frontman is reckless, but losing two... Certainly, Genesis would not survive another schism like that.

Smith, as a brilliant manager, is correct. And he'll be right for long. Each career, solo and band, reinforces the other.

Of course, I'm enjoying my unexpected solo triumph. Previously, I felt like the junior partner in Genesis. Years later, I discover I overestimated the boys' perception of me, as I learn from Mike's book: "If Phil had an idea, we listened." This is a revelation for Mr. Insecure. We'd never had such a discussion. We did not demonstrate emotional openness in front of one another.

About that tin of paint: "In the Air Tonight" is released as a single in the United Kingdom on January 5, 1981. Within a week, it's at number 36, and I'm on the BBC's weekly chart show, which unites the nation. How will I perform the song? I'm still uncomfortable standing there with a microphone, especially on television. So I'll play keyboards. My engineer, roadie, and factotum, Steve "Pud" Jones, responds, "I'll get a keyboard stand."

"Nah, seems like Duran Duran to me. Get a Black and Decker Workmate. That will do."

"OK. What will we play the drum machine on?"

"Um...a tea-chest?"

What about the paint tin? That's because we're going to rehearsal after practice, and the Top of the Pops producers are desperate to make this tea-chest look appealing. So Pud keeps adding small things.

"A paint pot...?"

So, yes, there is a DIY theme to that (in)famous Top of the Pops appearance. However, it has nothing to do with Andy's relationship with the decorator. That performance, and that paint pot, have returned to haunt me time and again.

While I'm wandering about the BBC studios, I speak with that week's host, Radio 1 DJ Dave Lee Travis. He sees one of the rehearsals for "In the Air Tonight" and says, "Cor, this is going to be massive."

"Are you sure?"

"Oh, yeah, this is going to be Top 3 next week."

And it is. Then it moves to number two. It appears to be heading straight to number one. Then John Lennon is shot, bringing everything into perspective. Life will never be the same. One of my heroes is no longer here.

Chapter 11: Hello, I Must Be Busy

Where were you on August 1, 1981 when MTV began broadcasting? What were you doing three days before Prince Charles married Lady Diana Spencer at St. Paul's Cathedral?

Throughout the 1980s, my videos, both solo and with Genesis, will be a staple on this revolutionary new television channel. I'll somehow end up becoming Charles and Di's go-to entertainer. No weddings or bar mitzvahs, but I'll play a few royal birthday parties, including an accidentally inappropriate divorce-themed performance around the time the heir to the throne married three people. Despite the importance of both Establishment and anti-Establishment institutions in my life, I find it difficult to recall my exact location and activities during the summer of '81 and during the subsequent decade.

I can't blame advancing age—I'm thirty years old today, six months after the release of Face Value—or rock'n'roll naughtiness. Simply put, I suppose I'm too busy to remember everything years later. And I am going to grow busier still. I'm so busy I don't even realize it. I only know that doing double duty as a solo artist and as a Genesis singer is unexpectedly demanding more of me than I could have imagined. Perhaps more than anyone thought. Few people before or subsequently have had both a tremendously successful solo career and a hugely successful band career.

Aside from the treasonous joking, I totally support The Prince's Trust's efforts. Charles founded the organization in late 1976 as a response to inner-city riots that reflected growing anger among British teenagers. Concerts and film premieres were previously common fundraisers for the Trust. Charles, aware of the power of a pop or rock event to connect with young and old, urged me to join as a trustee.

I contact Steve Hedges, one of Genesis' booking agents, and he sends me several cassette tapes of possible turns. If they're a covers band and do a good version of "Beat It," they're automatically on the shortlist. I eventually decide on an outfit called The Royal Blues. They sound good, can perform all current hits, and their name will make everyone happy at the palace. Later, I learn that they are the same band that performed at Charles' twenty-first birthday party. Thus far, so good.

The celebration will be hosted at Buckingham Palace, and I'm summoned approximately a month in before for a pre-party schedule walk-through. I meet with Charles's equerry and Nigel, The Royal Blues' briefcase-toting leader.

I recruited guitarist Daryl Stuermer to join me to make it seem more professional, and we prepared a set that covers all of the songs I can play with this smaller lineup. Unfortunately, that includes most of my saddest and most breakup-related tracks. This doesn't really get them dancing in the aisles. Even at this late stage in their marriage, and despite being relatively close to their inner circle, I'm perhaps the only person at Buckingham Palace that night who is unaware that Charles and Di are on the verge of splitting up.

Before I leave home, I commit two further cardinal sins. The first step is to approach the Queen and introduce myself. One must wait for the Queen to approach them. I also address her as "Your Highness" rather than "Your Majesty." Neither faux pas appears to upset her, and she's very nice, referring to me as her son's "friend," which tickles me to no end. I'm only getting to know her thoughts on the use of the 9/8 time signature in "Supper's Ready" when a beefeater interrupts.

As I eventually escape, driven forcefully towards something called "the Tower," I watch the Queen and Prince Philip dance to "Rock Around the Clock." This is not an image I will ever forget.

In July 1991, I had another contact with Princess Diana during her thirtieth birthday dinner at the Savoy. Again, I'm booked as the entertainment, and I play a set of completely inappropriate songs, including "Doesn't Anybody Stay Together Anymore." I sit at her table and ask for her autograph, which is another no-no according to royal protocol. However, during this time, we appear to meet on a regular basis at Prince's Trust plays and other associated activities.

Return to 1981. A year that began with my unexpectedly successful first solo album concludes with Abacab, a chart-topping Genesis album that has changed things up a bit—it features songs that are generally shorter, punchier, and less synthesizer-heavy than what we've done previously. I'm in my forties, yet my Tiggerish passion for change and experience remains unabated. I won't be Eeyore for a while yet.

The beginning of 1982 offers additional change and challenges. Anni-Frid Lyngstad of ABBA pays me a visit at The Farm, dressed stunningly in a large fur coat. She's also going through a divorce with Benny Andersson.

She doesn't say much about it during our meeting at The Farm, except that she's picked me to assist her achieve her goal. She appears to have been listening to Face Value on repeat, so she believes I understand and can connect to what she is going through.

I tell her I can, and how much I adore her fur coat.

Sitting in the studio, Frida and I choose the songs, although she has some pre-booked tunes that exclude any debate. ABBA's management issued a worldwide request for compositions, and from the hundreds of answers, an eclectic collection was assembled. I've included one by my friend Stephen Bishop, and she's chosen a Bryan Ferry song; a Giorgio Moroder co-write that appeared on a Donna Summer album the previous year; a Dorothy Parker poem set to music by the guy who went on to found Roxette; a song that was the British entry for the 1980 Eurovision Song Contest; and a rework of my Face Value track "You Know What I Mean." Talk about a smorgasbord.

Frida bursts into tears, and we all want to hit him. And I'm mobbed—the entire Genesis road crew is there, including burly Geoff Banks, one of our boys with the telling nickname "Bison." We've all grown to like this lovely person, and we all feel protective. But cooler, more sober, less Scandinavian heads prevail, and we depart, despite Stig's response ruining the entire evening for us.

Something's Going On will do well, with the single "I Know There's Something Going On" being a success in several countries around the world (and a popular source of samples for hip-hop artists). But I'm quickly seeing that the producing game has its own quirks. Perhaps being a self-produced solo artist is the simpler option after all.

Pete was roaming around London clubs with Steve Strange, a New Romantic gadabout. He was not in good shape after partying all night and recovering all day. Pete was still asleep when I arrived at the studio for our session. But after he got up, I grabbed him and said, "Who's going to play drums for The Who now? I'd love to do it."

"Oh damn, we just asked Kenney Jones to do it."

It was a genuine offer, and I was slightly disappointed. I would have quit Genesis to join Pete, Roger Daltrey, and John Entwistle. It's the Who, man! I grew up with that band. I absolutely loved the energy, and I'm confident I could have done it successfully.

I jumped at the opportunity to follow in the footsteps of one, if not two, Bonhams. I spent a few weeks in Rockfield Studios in Wales, where I played on six of the eight tunes on Robert's album Pictures at Eleven. We had a lot of laughs between records. Here are some amazing folks, and I'm back in a band, albeit just for a short time. Robert's players are a gang of Brummies, all nice solid lads who aren't impressed by the Zep thing. Robert is trying to reinvent himself I understand.

I return home to Surrey and begin work on my second album. I don't have much to work with—the previous year, I went from Face Value to recording Abacab, producing John Martyn's Glorious Fool, touring with Abacab, and then onto the Frida and Robert albums. There hasn't been time for thinking or songwriting.

Then I began the divorce proceedings between Andy and me. Or they hit me. Legal letters appear to arrive with ponderous regularity. There are demands for a share of this or that fortune, which does not exist. Although Face Value made a lot of impressions and sales, it will be a long time before the record and publishing corporations, as is their business strategy, send up the royalties. I get along. When I arrive to collect Simon and Joely, they often appear to be shoved out the front door.

I'm trying to be calm, but I admit I'm on edge, and there's a lot of shouting. Shouting that will ring in the children's ears for many years.

Neither, it appears, was the listening audience. "Thru These Walls," released in October 1982 as the first single from my second solo album, Hello, I Must Be Going!, enters the UK charts at number 56. In America, it performs far worse—my steadfast supporter Ahmet's label does not even consider it worthy of publication. My reaction is one of disappointment and resignation, not alarm.

Fortunately, Motown saves me, as it had done so many times throughout my youth—as a teenager, the label and its performers were the soundtrack to my life, as filtered via The Action's setlist. To pay respect, I included a cover of "You Can't Hurry Love" on Hello, I Must Be Going!. I consider it one of the Supremes' forgotten songs, a bit of a dark horse; tracks like "You Keep Me Hangin' On" and "Stop in the Name of Love" seemed to receive the most spins and affection.

Genesis embarked on a two-month tour of America and Europe in August, before releasing Hello. It's a tour to promote a live album, Three Sides Live, of which Rolling Stone says, "Where once Genesis represented art-rock at its most fatuously spectacular, they now show how lean and compelling such music can be." On the tour, we aim to avoid fatuous art-rock, and I do my best to be concise and captivating. We're still attempting to keep it lean and interesting on a dreary Saturday in autumn 1982, despite Genesis' lineup doubling and the British weather doing their best to dampen our spirits.

On October 2, at Milton Keynes' National Bowl, Peter and Steve, who arrived late from South America, join us for a fourteen-song set. For the first time since 1975, Genesis' "classic" lineup will reunite for one night only, with Daryl Stuermer and drummer Chester Thompson rounding out the lineup.

Seven years after his departure, we all cheerfully chip in to help. The Bowl is crowded with 47,000 spectators for this once-in-a-lifetime event. Talk Talk and John Martyn pulled the short straw and had to open for us, and the relentless rain did its best to mar the occasion. We barely had time for a few lunchtime rehearsals during Genesis' recent Hammersmith Odeon shows, so the song selection is primarily from the Peter era, and the whole concept feels better on paper than it does in practice. But we had to giggle when Peter insists on coming out in a coffin during the introduction to "Back in New York City." Pete is normally dark and hilarious, but I'm not sure the audience understands that.

Overall, the fans are satisfied, as are the critics: "It most likely fell short of Genesis and Gabriel's expectations of perfection. But this was an unrepeatable bargain. —Sounds: "A reunion that is unlikely to occur again. Melody Maker calls it the year's biggest rock festival. More importantly, we prevented our friend from being imprisoned or worse, and we helped WOMAD survive to fight another festival. It becomes the largest annual event on the global music calendar.

After Milton Keynes I'm just home long enough to see "Thru These Walls" released as a single, and my second solo album comes out in November. Hello, I really must be going: I immediately begin on my first solo tour, which will last until February 1983.

This, I'm realizing, is what happens when you're a solo artist who also plays in a band. There is no time to pause and smell the roses, or reflect and process past failures.

There is still time for nervousness and apprehension. I've been touring with Genesis since 1970, so after twelve years, I need to put together another excellent band to help alleviate the tension of being "on my own." I put together The Phenix Horns, with Daryl on guitar, Mo on bass, Chester on drums, and Peter from Brand X on keyboards. The set list is equally strong. I have two albums worth of material to chose from. The hits remain hits, while the ones that weren't become something else live. "I Don't Care Anymore," for example, develops becomes a massive stage hit.

Or are my memories hazy since that's how I feel about the album? Fundamentally, Hello, I Must Be Going! does not tick many boxes for me, although I am aware that some tracks are very popular among fans. However, there are no particularly vivid memories of writing or recording it.

I do know what my second album achieved for my career. It earned me my first Brit Award nomination (British Male Artist) and my first

Grammy nomination (Best Rock Vocal Performance, Male) for "I Don't Care Anymore."

But how did it affect my art and heart? Not much. I got the second solo CD, Blues.

Back in the United Kingdom in early April 1983, I reconnected with Robert Plant. I return to Rockfield and play on six of the eight tracks of what will become The Principle of Moments, his second solo album. This time, Robert decides to go on tour, a six-week trip across North America. Would I like to join him? You bet I would. After the chaos of my day job—day jobs—going back to being just a drummer, sitting behind everyone else, will feel like returning home. And doing it for Led Zeppelin's former lead vocalist is an honor I wouldn't pass up. It's a muso gig, as far removed from my current pop gig as possible, and I seize the opportunity. It's the growth of a wonderful friendship. Some individuals, particularly rock stars, come and go in your life, but Robert has remained a loyal friend.

During this time, I am not only constantly away from home, but I am also traveling in numerous directions. Jill is accompanying me on many of these adventures—she like the Plant tour since it is her kind of music—but not all of them, and maybe not enough. But we are getting along like a house on fire. Love is still in the air.

In May 1983, I returned home short and saw Mike and Tony at The Farm. After all my running about, it's nice to be back with the boys. As we continue recording Genesis' self-titled twelfth album, now that our studio is fully operating, we have the luxury of leisure and improvisation. Mike plays with a new toy. He subsequently recounts the harsh rhythmic sound he creates: "I programmed that with the very first big Linn drum machine." And I did something that Americans would never do: I plugged it into my small guitar amplifier and blasted it up so loud that it was jumping up and down on the chair. The English excel at messing up sounds. That is a prime example. "It's just a terrible but wonderful sound."

He is not wrong. It's immediately effective. We all fall in love with it, and inspired, I give my best John Lennon impersonation, and a vocal cue from Grandmaster Flash and the Furious Five's "The Message," which includes the insane laugh.

And it is "Mama," the Genesis album's main track. Our biggest-ever UK hit, both timely and timeless, and an enduring stage classic. It is followed by "That's All," which opens with Tony's piano riff and goes on to become our first Top 10 record in the United States. Released in October 1983, the album is another U.K. number one and sells 4 million copies in the United States, making it our best-selling record at the time. At the moment, we are simply extremely fortunate. Whether it's my thing or the Genesis thing, it just keeps growing. One profile reinforces the other, and our tunes appear to be appealing to a growing number of listeners.

By February 1984, I'm looking a little greedy. Before Genesis had concluded our five-night stint at Birmingham's NEC, the final gigs of a four-month tour spent primarily in North America, I released a new solo single in the United States. At least at home, I do the right thing—"Against All Odds (Take a Look at Me Now)" isn't released in the United Kingdom until after the tour ends, at the end of March.

On the other hand, in 1983-4, I had so many other things going on that it didn't occur to me to consider how this release date affects that touring schedule, how this solo obligation affects that band commitment. I'm simply keeping my head down and getting on with it.

Hackford adores it. I haven't seen the script, but he believes the lyrics are already excellent for the major musical subject of his picture, which is still in production. So I try to put together a proper recording. The piano and orchestra are recorded in New York under the guidance of the great Arif Mardin (who has worked with everyone from Aretha Franklin to Queen); the drums and vocals are recorded at Music Grinder in Los Angeles. Arif is a beautiful man and an outstanding producer who can obtain great performances in the most effortless way. I'm excited to work with him; I want to impress, and he brings out the best in me.

I already have the most of the crucial lines, including the "take a look at me now" line. But Hackford tells me that his film is titled Against All Odds, so I use an approximation of that, "against the odds." Hackford, on the other hand, is precise: he insists that I title and sing "Against All Odds."

The director is overjoyed with the outcome, and I am also satisfied. In a relatively short period of time, I appear to have established myself as a writer capable of crystallizing emotional agony. I'm the Phil Collins of Genesis legend, but to a growing number of people, I'm the Phil Collins who wrote "In the Air Tonight" and "Don't Let Him Steal Your Heart Away," and who can compose with both spaciousness and dramatic, cinematic scope.

The song is far bigger than the film. It's now regarded as a model of the 1980s power ballad, a phenomenon in which the hair was enormous, the emotions were big, but the shoulder pads were the biggest of all. Barry Manilow recorded it on his album The Greatest Songs of the Eighties, and Bazza understands what he's saying.

After years of singing it live, I can't say I'm dragged back into sad memories every time. If I was in that much pain every night, I would be a kook. Onstage, you're just trying to sing it—stay in pitch and get the phrases correct. I don't always manage. "How can I just let me walk away / when all I can do is watch me leave"—I've sung it a few times, which is pretty impressive for a clanger.

A year after its release, "Against All Odds" is nominated for an Oscar for Best Original Song. Normally, the nominated artist performs the nominated song. But in 1985, the Academy decides to change things: songs will be sung by others.

The argument begins with a communication from my label or management to the Academy expressing our desire to stop in Los Angeles on our way to an Australian tour and perform on the show. Soon, the letters start flying back and forth. One is addressed to "Mr. Paul Collins." Eventually, Ahmet Ertegun writes to Gregory Peck, the Academy's president at the time. This has gone all the way to the top. I've been watching the Oscars since I can remember, and I'm a huge movie fan. I'm honored to be among this exclusive set of nominees. I don't intend to offend anyone by inviting myself to sing my song. But now I'm unintentionally in the midst of an Oscar collapse.

The Academy assigns "Against All Odds" to a dancer for lip-sync. To be fair, she's no ordinary dancer—Ann Reinking, the ex-partner of great choreographer Bob Fosse, is extremely experienced. None of this keeps the whole thing from being a pig's ear.

It's all quite unseemly by the time I go to LA, because it appears like I'm the one who has been writing the letters. I attend the awards presentation, and everyone in the industry is aware of the controversy. When Ms. Reinking arrives on stage to perform the song. Everyone turns to see how I respond. I'm simply ashamed by what she's done to the music and what they believe is my argument. Stevie Wonder wins with "I Just Called to Say I Love You." At least "Against All Odds" wins the 1985 Grammy for Best Pop Vocal Performance, Male.

Still, I had no idea it was nominated for a Grammy. I only discovered out when the award arrived in the mail. "What is this?" "Anything else for Paul Collins?"

Chapter 12: Hello, I Must Be Busy II

Let's go back a year, to after the Mama tour ended in February 1984 and I finished promoting "Against All Odds."

Simon and Joely are developing into wonderful children. That said, I'm all for hard work, so I'm a bit of a taskmaster with Simon's math homework during the school holidays. To encourage him, I purchased an old-fashioned Victorian-era school desk and chair for his bedroom. He sits with his back to the window, laboriously concentrating on his algebra while the sun shines outside. Sorry, mate. I thought I was being a responsible father. And algebra will undoubtedly prove useful later in life.

Why did Philip Bailey want me to produce his album? Apparently I'm the hot man. In addition, the Earth, Wind, and Fire horn players have informed him about working with me. Philip and I have met a few times, and happily, we have moved on from the unfortunate incident in which EWF's management mistaken me for the band's drug dealer. The first to appear is Monte White, the tour manager and brother of band leader Maurice White. Soon, all the band members come and depart in their limousines. Finally, the Phoenix guys arrive, searching for their assigned automobile. Monte, meanwhile, believes that this shady, lurking Englishman is the Horns' drug dealer. He notifies Don Myrick, the section's saxophone player and leader, that no one other than the horn players would be allowed in the automobile. But after he leaves, Don insists I join them, which I do, if reluctantly—the White brothers run a very tight ship.

We only managed to write one song together, and it comes right at the end of the sessions. We set out on this adventure and begin improvising. Philip begins guiding us, and I sing something about a "choosy lover," which becomes the working title. We record a rough and energetic take late at night so we can remember it the next day. The following morning, we like what we hear, and that's pretty much it. I'll compose the words, and it'll eventually be renamed "Easy Lover," and published as a duet between two Philips. The record reaches number two in America, but is held back by Foreigner's "I Want to Know What Love Is." It reaches number one in the United Kingdom at the same time as I'm cringing my way through Ms. Reinking's rendition of "Against All Odds" at the 1985 Academy Awards.

Frankly, I had no clue he respected me so much that he would entrust me with his latest record. I was already on board before I found out we'd be recording on Montserrat. Clapton is God, according to ancient 1960s graffiti, even if he is your rural neighbor and drinking buddy. Even if I had a crystal ball and could see the problems ahead, I would still have said yes.

Eric's earlier album, Money and Cigarettes (1983), did not do anything for me. His music was just beginning. To my ears, it lacked a certain fire. So I start telling Eric about the benefits of having a small home studio where he can write. Inspired, he creates a setup similar to mine at Hurtwood Edge. I don't think he's ever used it. I believe the concept is foreign to Eric at this point, and it is too complex for him to handle on his own. He just wants to play, but I want him to express himself rather than merely cover other people's tunes.

The gorgeous Jamie Oldaker plays drums, and Chris Stainton, a veteran waiter with Joe Cocker's Grease Band, plays piano. Donald "Duck" Dunn, a Stax bass player, is a member of the ensemble, and his playing and personality contribute to the overall sense of fun and occasion. This guy is a true legend, a member of the original Booker T. & the MGs, who backed Otis Redding at Monterey, Sam & Dave, Eddie Floyd, and so many more. I'd grown accustomed to bass players traveling with many basses and figured it was the bass player's equivalent of penis envy. I inquire why he just has one. "I used to have two," he adds in his Southern drawl, "but one went down with Otis," alluding to the 1967 plane disaster that killed Redding. He also states that he has never modified the strings. Oh, the good old days.

I follow Eric's lead, producing in a way that is appropriate for the songs he has written—music that do not include interminable guitar solos. At Hurtwood Edge, we had lengthy discussions on writing, and

I encouraged him to write more. However, it turns out that interminable guitar solos are exactly what his new label—burned by the dismal sales of Money and Cigarettes—has been hoping for. Neither the artist nor the producer got the memo. Perhaps the artist did, but he didn't tell the producer.

The "finished" album is sent to the label. The label then rejected them. They tie a rope around Eric's neck and bring him to Los Angeles, where he records fresh songs written by Jerry Lynn Williams, a Texas singer-songwriter. Lenny Waronker (president of Eric's American label) remains vigilant and oversees extra production.

It was my first experience with record business intervention, and I still have the bruises. Only after that year, when I'm still reeling from the accusation that Eric and I failed to deliver, do I comprehend why he might have been so distracted as to allow the label to dictate the creative parameters so firmly. I'm not aware that he and Pattie are splitting up, despite my personal friendship with both of them. To me, they are the ideal couple.

Suddenly, I'm not his producer, Genesis' singer, or a solo celebrity. I am not even his companion. I'm a kid again, the straggly fifteen-year-old who stood outside The Attic in Hounslow in 1966, waiting for a bus and hearing Cream shake the walls. Now, Eric Clapton wants to record in my very basic home studio. It's a great song, and he wants it to be the album's title track, so I better not mess it up.

Now we need to combine it. It's just him and the guitar, but I added a little synth to add ambiance, just sustained strings. Old Croft isn't a great mixing studio, but Eric enjoys what he hears. The album concludes with a coda reflecting on the demise of his and Pattie's marriage: "My love has gone behind the sun…"

It's a lovely way to end the album. All of this occurred after the LA intrusion, so I feel somewhat vindicated. Years later, Eric tells Mojo that "Just Like a Prisoner," one of our Montserrat tracks, was his best guitar performance in as long as he can recall. I'm glad I was there.

After finishing Behind the Sun, I started thinking about my third solo album. During 1984, I will develop ideas and record small demos. I have an idea of what I want to do: break out from this "love song" box that I've found myself in. I'll create a dancing record. Or at least an album with a few upbeat tracks.

The title of the new album, No Jacket Required, was inspired by a few instances. Jill and I are on vacation in Caneel Bay on St. John in the American Virgin Islands. We go to eat at the hotel's outdoor restaurant. When I get to the front of the line, the maître d' notifies sir that he requires a jacket.

"I don't have a jacket, pal. I'm on holiday. "In the Caribbean."

There are a couple of other vacationers ahead of us, and the husband turns around to give me the raised eyebrow. "Jacket required," jokes Dr. Reuben Addams of Dallas. I don't forget the phrase, nor do I forget Reuben or his equally wonderful wife Lindalyn.

During Robert's Principle of Moments tour, we stayed at the Ambassador East in Chicago. He's wearing a loud Williwear suit, and I'm wearing a brand-new leather jacket and trousers. We proceed to the hotel bar for a drink. The bartender advises sir that he requires a jacket.

"I am wearing a jacket."

"A suitable jacket, sir..." "Not leather."

I am in the middle of recording No Jacket Required at Townhouse when Bob Geldof calls. I've never met him, but he gets right to the point: "Did you see the news?"

"No, I've been here working." When you're in the studio, you're completely isolated from the outside world; you're "in the woods," as Quincy Jones would say. Geldof tells me about Michael Buerk's BBC News broadcast on the Ethiopian famine. He then discusses his proposal for an all-star charity single. "We have to do something, and I need a famous drummer, and you're the only one I can think of."

He cites Midge Ure and George Michael, but that's it. A few short days later, on Sunday, November 25, 1984, I went down to SARM Studios—formerly Island Studios on Basing Street, Notting Hill, where Genesis recorded Foxtrot and Selling England and mixed The Lamb—to join the good and the great of the mid-80s British pop scene.

It is nerve-racking. Spandau Ballet, Bananarama, Status Quo, U2, Sting, and Culture Club are all in attendance. The majority of the music has already been recorded, so all that remains is for me to lay down the drums today, followed by all of the vocals. I have to come up with a drum part on the moment, while the best Smash Hits featured pages hover, watching and/or doing make-up (and that's just the men). However, fear might motivate you to perform better. I look around, and there is a warm sense of respect among the musicians in the room. This is gratifying, but also frightening, because I have not been told what is expected of me. Geldof just says, "Start here and play whatever you want." I perform my drum track, and there is applause. When I enter the control room, Midge exclaims, "That was great." I'll say, "Let me do it one more time." "No, we don't need to do it again." "Oh, OK..."

That was it—one take.

I meet Bono for the first time and start talking to Sting. The former cop and I click. Remembering that I have an album to finish, I ask Sting if he can help me out with some singing. He ends up singing background vocals on "Long Long Way to Go" and "Take Me Home," alongside Helen Terry and Peter Gabriel.

No Jacket Required is released on January 25, 1985, a week before my thirty-fourth birthday. Why is there a red face on the sleeve? Because it's a popular record, club-friendly, and upbeat. The sweat beads on my forehead are made up of both sweat and glycerin. The music and thoughts are genuine, but the cover, I admit, need just a hint of phoniness to make me appear hot and worried. I am not sure why—I have scarcely stood still for three years.

I only know this because I checked Wikipedia. In the eye of the tornado, and for years following, I couldn't care less about chart success or sales figures. I'm basically jogging in place.

These are the years when I'm everywhere, all the time, dominating the airwaves, MTV, the charts, and even the bloody Oscars. You can't get away from me even if you turn on the television or radio. If you take a charitable approach, I merely write a large number of hits. If you take a pragmatic approach, me and my music will not stop.

The No Jacket Required tour begins on February 11, 1985, at the Theatre Royal in Nottingham. I'll be touring the world for five months and eighty-three gigs with a band I call The Hot Tub Club. Multiple nights at London's Royal Albert Hall and other venues in the United Kingdom, followed by the rest of Europe, Australia, and Japan, before a lengthy run in America—including three nights at Universal Amphitheatre in Los Angeles and two nights at Madison Square Garden—through the summer.

Is it not enough? Don't worry, another project, single, and inescapable Phil Collins song are on the way.

"Separate Lives" is another American number one, bringing my total to more than anyone else in 1985, and Stephen is nominated for an Oscar. That same so-called award season, No Jacket Required wins three Grammys and I receive my first Brit Awards for Best British Album and Best British Male Artist. But, even before those award events in early 1986, I'm back in Genesis world by the end of 1985, working on the album that will become Invisible Touch. And off we go again.

But first, during my summer holiday in 1985, I receive a phone call from the workplace. It appears that the popular American detective series Miami Vice wants me to do a cameo in one of their episodes. The show featured "In the Air Tonight" in its debut episode, and it worked so well that it became known as the theme music. In truth, Fred Lyle, the series' music producer, has used my song numerous times.

So I do, and we have fun. Don Johnson is extremely pleasant to me, and my female counterpart is Kyra Sedgwick, Kevin Bacon's wife. Even Jill has a role in the party scene. It's all over in 10 days, and I'll be home for the summer.

The phrase "workaholic" is regularly used to characterize myself. I'll reject it till I'm red in the face and glycerine sweat runs down my brow. Simply put, I am asked to do things that I cannot possible refuse.

I am not producing Duran Duran, collaborating with Boy George, or touring with Cyndi Lauper. I'm not looking for another Top of the Pops slot or another zero on my bank balance. Robert, Eric, John, Philip, and Frida are folks I grew up with, admire, and/or look good in fur coats. I consider these people to be true artists and icons. Working with them is an honor. That is the cause.

Nonetheless, I recognize that in some circles, I represent the high eighties. But I'm not a yacht-driving, flashy buyer of Ferraris and penthouses. There are some dodgy suits, but everyone had them in the 1980s. So what if Brett Easton Ellis' Patrick Bateman sees myself as the embodiment of everything great about that joyful, gaudy decade's music? He's a psychopath.

One of the best aspects of this time is that Jill can travel with me and have fun, which strengthens our bond even more. She never complains about the amount of work I do. Joely and Simon are spending much of their time in Vancouver with their mother, and I check in on them as often as can. They always appear joyful, which makes me happy. But I miss so many special moments with them. Looking back, I can hardly believe it. If there is a downside to success, that's it.

Where were you on August 4, 1984, in the midst of the Los Angeles Summer Olympics, tarnished by the Eastern Bloc boycott, which was a tit-for-tat reprisal for the American-led boycott of the 1980 Moscow games?

We held the reception in our garden at Old Croft, where an all-star band performed into the night. Eric, Gary Brooker, Robert Plant, Stephen Bishop, Ronnie, Daryl, and Chester—so many wonderful friends pitched in. Even the unexpected appearance of the Dyno-Rod man—someone had clogged the downstairs toilet—could not dampen the mood.

We spent our honeymoon aboard a yacht in the Aegean, sailing along the Greek and Turkish coasts. My professional and personal lives were both thriving.

And where were you when Live Aid happened July 13, 1985? I'm familiar with that as well.

Chapter 13: The Great Brain Robbery

Daddy's home! In the summer of 1985, following Live Aid, I made every effort to return to being a family man. I normally have Simon and Joely for the lengthy school holidays, and since they live in Vancouver the rest of the year and I'm constantly busy elsewhere, these summer months when we can get together are sacred. Even though Joely, Simon, and I communicate frequently, each visit is a surprise. They both have larger personalities, are more fashion-conscious, cognizant of their haircuts, and, of course, grow taller.

I have numerous home films from that era, and it's amazing to hear their changing accents. Joely, in instance, steadily transitions from prim and English to more mid-Atlantic. They're both developing into nice young people with good manners, but with these changes come problems—problems I wish I'd been present to share. Both my geographically separated children and I are experiencing growing pains.

"Home" is now at Lakers Lodge in Loxwood, West Sussex. We decided to relocate from Old Croft while I recorded No Jacket Required in London. Jill took on the big work of locating us a new home while I was otherwise occupied in the studio. It wasn't quite the same as my mother buying a new home and moving the family in on one of my father's nine-to-five days, but it was close.

The property comes with a tiny crew, a middle-aged couple named Len and Joyce Buck, who have lived on the grounds for 25 years. Len is a modest and rightfully proud old-school gardener who knows when to reap and sow. Joyce is a housekeeper and employer.

August also marks my and Jill's first wedding anniversary, so there's even more motivation to stay close to heart and home. She has generally accompanied me as I have moved from project to project, nation to country, and collaboration to collaboration during the last four years. Coming on the road was exciting for her, albeit not as overpowering as it could have been, given her entertainment background: her father was a Hollywood outfitter who made outfits for the rich and famous, and her mother was an actress and dancer. When I was recording a clip of "Over the Rainbow" as a little coda to Face Value and couldn't remember the lyrics, Jill called her mother, who knew the lyricist, Yip Harburg. He dictated them to her on the phone. As if directly from Dorothy's mouth.

We have mutually agreed that having children is not an option for us right now and will not be for several years. First, we have Joely and Simon to consider. They're still young—she was born on August 8, so I usually get to celebrate Joely's birthday with her during the school holidays; on the other hand, I usually just miss Simon's birthday, which is on September 14—and we don't want to complicate things any further until they're ready to deal with even more change.

But this divided, worldwide dispersed family—something we'll laugh about years later, when it's even more fragmented and scattered—is more than just a standard "mum and dad got separated" scenario. It's tough, but I strive to keep things calm, functional, and, most importantly, loving.

Anyway, the summers are a break for me, but not so much for Jill. Suddenly, she becomes a mother. She's really excellent at it, but it's not without difficulties as the kids strive to bond with an unavoidably absent father and a new mother figure. that they're older, Simon and Joely tell me that it was more difficult than they made it appear at the time, especially during the brief period that they lived back in the UK with Andy. In fact, Simon tells me that he used to run away from primary school in Ealing because he despised it so much. Or perhaps he despised his life so much. Regardless, I can't help but feel guilty.

No one told me this at the time. However, I now realize that I have photographic evidence. Simon is at the end of the line in a school photo, sitting a good meter away from his classmates. It could not be more symbolic if he was holding a vinyl copy of Face Value under his arm. I still wince when I see that photo of my tiny boy.

Jill and I will have our time after Joely and Simon have gone to bed. We'll watch a movie or talk, but as they get older, their bedtimes increase later, and our time alone together shrinks—as it does for most couples with children.

I've gotten used to bargaining with Andy over when I can have the kids. Divorce may be brutal to children, who are often used as pawns in adult games. They hear one side of a discussion, the shouting, the phone slamming down, and then have to listen to Mum or Dad scold the other. It's terrible enough that their parents are no longer living together; they don't want to hear them argue now that they're separated. But wisdom comes with age, and I believe I now hold a master's degree in divorce and people management. I'll come to regard my adult life as forty years of negotiation.

After my summer vacation, I am eager to return to work. I don't resent this in any way. Unlike my father, who was dissatisfied and, I believe, permanently damaged by the job he was obliged to perform, what I do for a profession is what keeps me alive. I enjoy my job.

With the kids safely back in Canada, Genesis reunited at The Farm in October to begin work on the album that would become Invisible Touch. Now that I'm at Lakers Lodge, Mike, Tony, and I all live close together and can drive to the studio in ten minutes.

If I ever decided to leave Genesis in favor of my solo career, now would be the time, with the tailwind of No Jacket Required still blowing hard. But, at the same time, I have missed the men. Tony and Mike have become more lovable with time, which contradicts the usual rock-band storyline. Tony, who was formerly shy and difficult to talk to, has grown into a wonderful friend who is both humorous and intelligent. He is a different person, especially after a glass of alcohol. Mike has also loosened up.

So I've missed them, and our unique studio working style. We have no plans, so we go in and improvise. We play. It's not as if John and Paul each bring a song. I don't aware of any other band that works the way we do, sitting around and jamming until something comes together. Every other band appears to be more organized—or boring—than that. I thought, "I can't do this anywhere else." We've got something special here.

We begin with a blank sheet of paper and the magnificent large control room that has been erected at The Farm since we last recorded here. We also have a live room for my drums, but we are beginning to use drum machines more than on any prior album. It frees me to write and sing the songs.

The song "Invisible Touch" is one example. Mike's guitar riff prompts me to sing: "She seems to have an invisible touch..." This motion "takes control and slowly tears you apart..." This person is dangerous and destabilizing. I'm Andy, and this is Lavinia. Someone who will come in and fuck up your life, guy, is the line I will end up singing onstage, much to the audience's delight and my children's chagrin.

But "Invisible Touch" isn't bitter or angry; it's about acceptance. Simon often laughs when I tell him, "She seems to have an invisible touch..." after a failed relationship. He looks to have comparable relationships as I do. Even with my son Nic and the females he meets at school, I tell him there are some people he should not go out with. But you find yourself drawn to them.

Despite the haunted, fever-dream nature of the lyrics, "Invisible Touch" has a bounce to it, influenced by "The Glamorous Life," a massive American dance song from 1984 by Prince's sometime drummer and co-singer Sheila E. It's one of my favorite Genesis songs, and when it was released as the album's first single in May 1986, it became our first—and only—number one hit in the United States. In fact, it is the first of five American Top 5 songs from Genesis' bestselling album, Invisible Touch, which was released one year after my bestselling album, No Jacket Required.

Between the completion of recording Invisible Touch and starting the next tour, I reconnect with Eric. We appear to have both been forgiven for Behind the Sun, as I am now allowed to drum on and co-produce Tom Dowd's upcoming record. It will be named August in honor of his son Conor's birth month. We record in Los Angeles, under the watchful supervision of Lenny Waronker, to ensure that there is enough of guitar. August becomes Eric's best-selling album to date, which we can attribute to improved song selection, Waronker's correctness, my superior production skills, or a magical mix of the three. We follow that energy into a series of live gigs across Europe and America, during which I join Eric's touring lineup. It's great fun performing with Eric, Greg Phillinganes, and Nathan East—we call it The Heaven Band—and it's a nice, peaceful preparation to what's coming up.

The Invisible Touch tour begins in September 1986, with three nights in Detroit's 21,000-capacity Joe Louis Arena. It won't be over until ten months and 112 shows.

We go throughout the world, staying three nights here, four nights there, and five nights in Madison Square Garden. Days off on tour? Not particularly interested. I'll hang out at the hotel, maybe go to the movies, and not do much else. It's not because I'm worried about being disturbed by fans on the street; it's simply because I'm counting down the hours until that night's show. That is what I am here for. Alternatively, I sit in my room and listen to tapes of the previous night's show, examining the sound mix for any sloppiness or mistakes made by any of us onstage. Eventually, I'll grasp that every show has its own time and place.

Sometimes, at the recommendation of the greatest throat doctors rock'n'roll money can buy, I'll go myself to the nearest steam room. Now that I'm playing so many performances, both solo and with Genesis, and increasingly in large settings, I'm afraid of losing my voice, and the steam is helping.

In Australia, our route matches that of Elton John. I spend an informative evening in his Melbourne dressing room. He's performing with the Melbourne Symphony, and it'll be broadcast all over Australia. Elton throws a tantrum because he believes he has lost his voice. It appears he is willing to cancel the event, regardless of the impact on the dozens of orchestral players and tens of thousands of supporters. He summons his limo, is driven around the parking lot at a slow pace, but eventually returns to the stage.

After the show, in his dressing area, I tell him that I only noticed a small vocal wobble in one location, during "Don't Let the Sun Go

Down on Me." He's happy to hear it, but I think a tantrum is just a tickly tonsil away.

For me, it's an enlightening interlude. Most of the time, the audience misses these subtleties—I scarcely noticed, but I knew he was hoarse. You should consider twice before allowing a scratchy throat turn into a diva-style cancellation. With 20,000 spectators, there are few reasons that will suffice, short of actually dying in the steam room prior to the event.

In July 1987, the Invisible Touch tour concludes with a return home. However, only six of the 112 shows are in the United Kingdom, so we'd better hit it out of the ballpark. Those parks are the Scottish and English national football stadiums, Hampden in Glasgow and Wembley in London, respectively.

For a football fan, these are memorable moments. At Hampden, we were allowed to use the trophy room as our dressing room, which reminded me of where England and Scotland played. "I wonder if Jimmy Greaves sat here."

After most gigs, I come down to earth with a thump. But there's something strange about Wembley that I've never felt elsewhere. This site was so essential to me in my early years that walking around the stadium, on the turf, is an incredible feeling.

I was twelve years old in 1963 when the Great Train Robbery occurred. I recall skimming the headlines in Mum and Dad's newspaper the day after the heist. I knew it was crucial. Most of Britain seemed to admire the ingenuity of the fifteen-strong band of criminals who stopped the midnight Glasgow to London mail train in such a simple way—by tampering with the signal lights—and then stole its cargo of banknotes worth £2.6 million. In today's money, that is equivalent to around £50 million. really, really princely.

Following their capture, the gang members received excessively hefty prison sentences. The swinging sixties were just getting started, and the country's atmosphere was shifting, so the common perception was that they had been made an example of by the British Establishment. One of the convicted criminals, Ronnie Biggs, dubbed "the tea boy" by the gang, escaped from London's Wandsworth prison and fled to Paris, then Australia, before settling in Rio de Janeiro, where he became well-known as the famous train robber. Almost forty years after the heist, he returned to the United Kingdom and faced punishment in 2001.

Two of the gang's main members escaped the country before Biggs, fleeing to Mexico, where they became folk heroes among certain people back home. One was Bruce Reynolds, the gang's commander. The other was his first mate, Buster Edwards.

So, one day in 1987, I received an offer from a film firm. They were filming a film based on the life of Buster, who, after returning from Mexico skint and homesick with his family, spent nine years in jail before going straight and establishing a flower booth outside Waterloo station in London.

According to the filmmakers, Buster's narrative was a romance. Throughout his life of minor crime and jail time, he and his wife June were inseparable. They wanted to tell the couple's narrative, with the Great Train Robbery serving as a backdrop.

Would I consider taking the role?

Of sure, I would consider it. I could have been over acting in my teens and the late 1960s—I'd had more than a few negative experiences on screen (and on the cutting room floor), and I was more interested in making it as a musician—but that was a long time ago. A new creative challenge sounds enticing.

Why me? Apparently the director, David Green, was watching TV one night when my episode of Miami Vice aired. Within minutes, his wife told him, "There's your Buster."

Immediately after I emerge from make-up, producer Norma Heyman, David Green, Julie, and I am invited to lunch at Wembley Studios. I'm still wearing the prosthetic nose, and this is my first meeting with Julie. The goal is to see whether we can connect. She's delighted to meet me and my artificial nose, and I immediately fall for her. She's so appealingly humorous, all of her brilliant Acorn Antiques and Wood and Walters sketches come pouring back. But a little "falling" is acceptable, because leading men and women must have chemistry, right? Enthralled by such an experienced, and gorgeous, actress, I'm privately concerned about whether my old acting talents will be adequate. I do not want to let Julie down.

As if the embarrassment of having to meet her with a shoddy artificial nose wasn't enough, Green and Heyman suggest we go to a rehearsal. Specifically, the practice of a kissing scene. Under normal circumstances, this would very likely make me extremely happy. But, since there wasn't much kissing required in Oliver! or Calamity the Cow, I'm not sure how you stage-kissed. What are the parameters? Are there tongues? What if my nose falls off?

As I try to get my head, mouth, and nostrils around this, the director leans in and barks instructions: "Harder, closer..." Remember to keep your nose clean if you're married. Green and Heyman are shouting at me from barely a foot away. This is all really intimidating.

Finally, we're done, and Julie isn't too traumatized. Fortunately, the nose is blown, and we can film without it.

This is when Danny Gillen comes into my life. Belfast-born and a huge man with a great heart, he's employed to pick me up every morning at 5:30 in West Sussex, take me to various sites in London, and care after me throughout the day—not least to make sure none of Buster's old "pals" decide to come say hello—before driving me home. Throughout it all, we became inseparable friends and have remained such to this day. From Buster to, there will be many experiences and scrapes involving anything from paparazzi to over-eager fans to junkie Australian robbers, which I will only be able to handle with Danny's persistent assistance.

I must admit that playing Buster Edwards is not difficult for me. I assume he is an extension of The Artful Dodger, a cockney wide-boy. But there are storms off-screen.

Between October 15 and 16, 1987, a massive storm battered England. That night at Lakers Lodge, I felt the solid Georgian mansion shake and the cataclysmic crash of trees being blown down. I lose approximately twenty in all, but others are far worse off—an estimated

15 million trees are destroyed across the country, causing £5 billion in damage in today's money.

The next morning, Danny and I are unable to go to the film location in London because most of the roads in rural Sussex are blocked by fallen trees. Finally, late in the day, we find a way through, and what we see is horrific: trees smashed like matches in downtown London, devastated buildings, flattened cars, and lives uprooted everywhere. We do our best with the scenes that day, but everyone's mind is elsewhere: the majority of the cast and crew have had their homes damaged and are attempting to contact relatives, emergency services, utility providers, and insurers.

Finally, we reshoot the sequence a few months later, when Julie is nearly seven months pregnant. However, we manage to get around the elephant in the room.

Buster's partner-in-crime, Bruce Reynolds, attends the same cast and crew party and occasionally stops by while we film on site. We get fairly friends, and one day, when we're shooting at a location identical to Leatherslade Farm, where the actual criminals holed up after the crime, Bruce comes up and says, "This is a great site, Phil. "I'll need to remember this address." He appears to still be open for business.

Meanwhile, the Buster soundtrack has been experiencing its own upheaval. The filmmakers' first thought was to have me sing the theme tune. They want the Phil Collins package, which includes acting, singing, and writing. I am firm. "No, I don't want people to think of me as a singer when they see me acting." I'm taking this work seriously. It'll be a difficult gig even without my band/pop character making an appearance on film.

I offer a few options. I know a few people that can supply accurate period music. I just met one of my heroes, Lamont Dozier of Holland-Dozier-Holland Motown, while on the No Jacket Required tour. He came backstage in LA, and we exchanged love, phone numbers, and promises to work together. George Martin, the Beatles producer, is also my dear friend.

I refuse to sing "Loco in Acapulco" because it will appear in the middle of the film. I eventually invite The Four Tops to create them with Lamont. I have the daunting task of singing the melody to Levi Stubbs, one of the most remarkable voices of the 1960s. I'm under a lot of pressure to sing "Two Hearts." Eventually, I answer, "Okay, but it won't be until the end credits, right? I want people to evaluate if I can act before they hear me sing.

I go to see a rough cut of the film, and there it is, my demo playing over a beautiful goodbye kiss between Julie and me. I protest. However, because it works so well in the picture, I am stuck with it. So we re-record "A Groovy Kind of Love," with symphonic great Anne Dudley producing, and release it as a single.

To paraphrase a much greater sixties-set British film: I was simply supposed to blast off the bloody doors. Instead, I wind up with another number one record in the United Kingdom and the United States, and a lot of criticism for performing another middle-of-the-road sixties cover, even if it was only for a movie.

But, in the grand scheme of things, what matters? I'm thrilled to see Buster Edwards emerge as a new type of folk hero after the film's release in November 1988. He and June are a great couple who became firm friends with Jill and me, visiting Lakers Lodge a few times a year. Buster kills suicide in 1994, and I'm crushed. The newspapers had horrific stories about him, but I believe he was just depressed and bored. He'd remark to me, "Fuck, Phil; I'm selling flowers outside Waterloo Station. "There's no excitement like before..."

Buster is a classic small British film: a nostalgic, romantic romp set in the swinging 1960s that performs well at the box office in the United Kingdom. Julie and I were a perfect casting match, and I'm very happy with the experience. Finally, I have my first leading role.

Prior to its debut, my performance receives favorable advance notices, so I'm excited to be able to do something with my newfound (and undoubtedly brief) cinematic clout. In another aspect of my life, I am still a trustee of The Prince's Trust. Having grown close to Prince

Charles and the Princess of Wales, I do the obvious and invite them to attend the film's premiere in support of the Trust.

But then the tabloid press enters. During the Great Train Robbery, one of the gang members coshed the train driver, Jack Mills. He died seven years later, but others claimed he was never the same after the crime. The newspapers carry items like "Royal Film Glorifies Violence," and then there's an embarrassing backpedaling.

Bounding onstage at the Globes in Los Angeles to accept the prize for "Two Hearts" (Best Original Song), I exclaim, "This is great for me. This is from a British film called Buster, which went nowhere, owing primarily to the distribution corporation. But, as I always say, "forgive and forget." "Or at least pretend to."

Hearing this, one voice laughs. Cleese recognizes one of his Basil Fawlty lines. That makes my night: I made John Cleese laugh.

Chapter 14: Faxgate

It is the morning following the previous affair.

The emotional turmoil has left me depleted. The rejection isn't what's killing me. It's a loss. It's no surprise that at the end of the We Can't Dance tour in Wolverhampton on November 17, 1992, my mind isn't completely focused. The massive run of globetrotting concerts may have concluded, but I'm still all over the place—a feeling exacerbated by a bizarre trip to Neverland.

That December, I'm in Los Angeles to present the Billboard Awards, which I've never done before. Michael Jackson will be the night's biggest winner. He has swept the board with Dangerous. Furthermore, it's the tenth anniversary of Thriller, and Billboard wants to commemorate its ever-increasing sales numbers.

Unfortunately, Jackson is on tour the day after the awards, so I plan to pre-record my presentation of the trophies at his Neverland property in Santa Barbara.

When we finally get out of the limo, two greeters dressed in Disney-esque outfits greet us. Muzak plays in the grounds, as children run around the on-site amusement park.

We are escorted into the house and parked in his living room while we wait for the maestro to come downstairs. He has Thriller-era images on the wall, and family portraits. There's also a large oil picture of Jackson surrounded by animals and birds, with the King of Pop channeling St. Francis of Assisi.

Michael eventually descends and introduces himself. He is really lovely and friendly. All memories of the strange things I've heard vanish in an instant, and I don't blink when he asks Lily and Jill to play upstairs in his toy room. He and I walk to his studio complex, where camera teams are setting up—aside from the Billboard Awards team, he has his own team that films everything he does for his archives.

I apologized profusely to Jill, explaining that Lavinia was a one-time occurrence, and resolved to be a better, more faithful husband.

In my studio at the top of the house, while I consider the beginnings of the songs that may comprise my next solo album, I am experiencing different, darker thoughts. If it wasn't Lavinia, I'd be able to get it out of the way, remove the thoughts, and bury the pain. But, this is Lavinia. She is something exceptional. What is the bitter truth? I'm completely bewildered. Could my life's first love be the last?

The emotions that drive these new songs are identical to those that gave Face Value its intensity, impact, and, I hope, resonance. They are me, exposed and raw. On my first solo album and this, my fifth, I put everything out there. In the long run, this is why Face Value and Both Sides are my two favorite albums, whereas No Jacket Required falls short for me.

Specifically, on both sides, the wrath and hurt of Face Value have been replaced by feelings of regret, grief, and nostalgia. Lyrically, I believe I hit some of those emotions dead on. I adore how simple and pure the tunes are.

As I write, I make a decision. Nobody else will perform or record these songs because they are so personal and close to home. This is private, and I plan to keep it that way for as long as possible. The irony, of course, is that if I've done my job correctly and written movingly from the heart, I'm afraid that as soon as Jill hears Both Sides, our marriage will collapse.

I suppose that by keeping the development and recording of these songs to myself, I'm trying to postpone that moment for as long as possible.

I play all of the instruments, record the vocals, and refine my home recordings until they're nearly ready for release before bringing them to The Farm to add drums. There, I'll hold them close to my breast by creating the record myself, and doing so quickly. The musicianship may be described as amateurish. Or, better, intimate. But that works for these songs; it's part of their appeal.

While I am aware that writing these songs will have far-reaching consequences for my personal life, I am unaware that recording them in this manner will have an equally catastrophic influence on my professional life. That will come a bit later. However, the record is currently complete.

Then some breathing space before I go public with Both Sides. In early 1993, the phone rings with an alluring invitation: Stephan Elliott, a young Australian director who had seen Miami Vice, wants me to play the lead in a grim comedy called Frauds, about a twisted insurance inspector who terrorizes the life of a couple he suspects of fraud.

Between finishing recording Both Sides and its release, I head to Sydney for the shoot. It's fantastic fun and a refreshing change of pace after the We Can't Dance tour and what's been going on back home. Hugo Weaving is my co-star, and he'll soon rise to prominence in The Matrix series, while Elliott goes on to direct the brilliant, ABBA-inspired musical The Adventures of Priscilla, Queen of the Desert.

"Both Sides of the Story" is the first single from Both Sides, released in October 1993. The song is about seven minutes long and appears on the album. Even when cut for radio, it still lasts five and a half minutes. The Americans like "Everyday" as the first single because "it's more like what Phil Collins does." I dig in my heels. I don't care if this record isn't as successful as my last four. It is not intended to be. It's a fiercely, proudly personal record, created entirely from my screenplay and specs. It's my heart on my sleeve, as ugly and messy that may be.

I do not see Both Sides as a public declaration that I have ended my second marriage. This is clearly not Jill's message. Rather, it is an honest description of the agony I have been going through. I'm only acknowledging what happened in the only way I know how.

Anyway, I have more serious worries. To be really honest, I've realized that my marriage to Jill has ended. I've ruined everything, and I don't see a way back. I feel terrible for Lily, who is attempting to make sense of the catastrophe her father has created. I'll always be sorry about that. I know that admitting to these thoughts will destabilize Jill and Lily's life, so I make the difficult decision to take the coward's path: I say nothing.

They're long and hard sets that start to tax you right away. I approach the stage through a phony door, hang up my coat, and seat down at what appears to be a pile of trash but contains drums. Drummer Ricky Lawson, who first joined the band, appears with a kit of pads hidden inside his vest. There is a call-and-response drum piece, and we easily transition into "I Don't Care Anymore." And we are off. I'm enjoying pouring myself into the performances. Distraction is certainly good, as is the release of energy and emotion. Receiving enthusiastic responses night after night never fails to brighten me up.

On April 26, I fly into Geneva. I have a gig tonight in Lausanne, Switzerland's fourth largest city, which is located on the banks of Lake Léman. I'll be in Lyon the day after tomorrow, and the tour will end three days later in Paris. I'm scheduled to perform three gigs at the Palais Omnisports stadium, each with a capacity of 20,000.

As with every other airport when we land, we are greeted by cars driven directly onto the tarmac, generally carrying a local record label employee or something similar.

So we deplaned and divided into two groups. Two Renault Espace vans with drivers were waiting as scheduled. And this incredibly beautiful woman. Girl, truly.

She is quite smart, dressed officially in a gray skirt suit, and very attractive. She introduces herself as Orianne—an uncommon name, I think—and says Michael Driberg, the local Swiss music produceemployeded her to translate during our stay in Lausanne.

She is not a professional translator, despite popular belief. Orianne is twenty-one and works in the Geneva offices of Capital Ventures, an investing firm. But, because Driberg knows her and knows she speaks good English, he asked whether she would pick me up from the airport, transport me to the hotel, escort me to the concert, and then deliver me home again, all while satisfying my linguistic needs.

We arrive at the very magnificent Beau-Rivage. Get out, check in, and I'll take this moment to admire the full glory of this beautiful woman. Half my age, half Asian, and half a world apart. But numbers signify nothing.

I have about an hour until soundcheck, so Orianne arranges for the driver to come back and pick me up for the gig. Danny and I go upstairs, and for the first time in our whole travel career, we have adjoining rooms. We open the doors between suites and talk hard.

I manage to unpack, gather my thoughts, and realize I have a job that night. We arrive at the lobby at the scheduled time and find Orianne waiting, still dressed professionally but smiling sweetly.

Back in the car, we head to the Patinoire de Malley venue for the gig, then into the dressing room. Orianne hangs around since it is her job to look after me. It quickly becomes clear that she is not only attractive but also intelligent. Nothing has happened except in the remote reaches of my naïve, wishful imagination, but I'm already plagued by guilt, an old Collins chestnut.

Following soundcheck, I brush up on my locally obtained stage patter. French, German, Italian, Japanese—everywhere we play, I prepare a brief spiel in the native tongue to show respect and nod to the locals. I've always done that, just like Peter did in Genesis.

Carol asks me, "Do you want to do your French now?"

I'm trying to be casual. "Ah, yeah, could you get Orianne?"

"Yeah, she's lovely, isn't she?"

Orianne enters, sits opposite me, and asks, "What would you like to say?"

We practice concert lines like "Bon soir…" But, yes, I may have put forth a little more effort that evening to master some portions. I honestly want to drag it out. But I can no longer detain her. And toward the end, I ask, "Have you got a boyfriend?"

"What do you mean?"

"Have you got a boyfriend?"

"Yes."

"OK… But I'd love to take you out to supper.

She's a little flustered, but appears to agree. She swiftly gets to her feet and heads for the door. "But at least I said something," I believe, "and created some personal, non-work contact. " Just before she goes, I say, "I'll see you afterward, right?"

"Yes, I'll take you back to the hotel."

We do the show, and I'll admit that there is some pouting on my part. More so than usual. I'm trying to put on the best show possible. I may even have thrown a couple more athletic shapes than usual.

Because this is a massive ice hockey arena, there are multiple doorways leading from the arena floor to the hot dog vendors, bars, and souvenir stalls. During the show, I observe Orianne and a buddy standing by one of the doors closest to the stage. She's dancing a little, moving in sync with the music, and having fun. I am pleased as a schoolboy.

The show is ended, and I'm backstage getting changed. I ask Carol whether she has seen the translator girl. Carol, presumably with pursed lips, admits she has no idea where she is. Danny enters with the suitcases. Are I prepared to go? Not really. Where is the translator girl? Danny says he can't find her and that we must leave the property. Reluctantly, I return to the motel. It's fair to say my mood is down.

Danny calls the venue's back office from our adjoining rooms, responding to my casual but insistent request. "Is the translator girl around? The promoter's girl? "Oh, she is there?" Orianne appeared to have been waiting for us, but had missed us in the throng of 10,000-odd fans exiting the auditorium and a ten-strong band and thirty road crew rushing about their post-show business.

Orawan goes to acquire a phone number for her. Only later do I realize that in her haste to locate me the number, she left the dinner cooking on the burner. The food burns and the kitchen catches fire. Dad, not surprisingly, loses his rag. The phone rings one minute, and the fire alarm sounds the next. "It's OK," Orawan says amid the din, smoke, and flames, "I have Phil Collins on the phone!"

She gives me the phone number of Orianne's best friend, Christophe, with whom she is currently out. I call, and Christophe hands her the phone.

I understand that in the cold light of the printed page, this can all come across as a little, well, stalkerish. What shall I say? She already had me by the heart.

Danny and I reserve a prime table at our hotel's highly acclaimed restaurant and promptly order a nice bottle of wine. We sit, sip, and wait. And we wait. The waiter hovers. "Another bottle of wine, sirs?" I'm feeling good, and not just because of the Chateau Orianne.

Another waiter walks up. "Monsieur Collins, there's a phone call for you."

It's Orianne. She claims she can't come. Why not?

"Because my boyfriend heard about you and he hit me."

I later learn that she was breaking up with him. But right now, he has punched her in the face, and she has a thick lip. I convey my fury and sorrow, and I'm considering dispatching Danny to deal with this fucker. I tell her I don't care how she looks; she should just come to the restaurant.

"Maybe later."

Danny and I eat and then go up to our neighboring rooms. Eventually, the phone rang. Orianne is in the lobby, alongside Christophe. He's a beautiful large person that I'll become very close to. He wants to make sure his best buddy is okay, that she isn't playing about with some jerk, especially after the night she's had. Perhaps he's also heard that the Ceveys' kitchen has caught fire.

The four of us meet for a drink in my room. Christophe ultimately looks at me and says, "Phil." You are a wonderful guy. I will leave you alone. But I will be waiting in the automobile."

For the next few days, I feel like a dog with two tails. But at the same time, I'm about to travel to Paris. And in Paris, I'll meet my wife and our five-year-old daughter, who are coming in from London.

What did I do? Well, I know what I did. I have deceived my wife and child. Again. And I've set sail for dangerous unexplored waters." Meet Phil Collins' new mysterious lover. "She is young enough to be his daughter." Ticks all midlife crisis boxes.

My affair with Lavinia had already pulled the rug out from under my marriage, and I was kidding myself if I believed I could make things right with Jill after that. This makes dealing with guilt no easier, and it will continue to be difficult for years to come. My love life is a stew of strife, of which I am not proud.

From my hotel room window in Paris, I watch Jill and Lily exit the limo. I feel like an absolute shit.

If my marriage to Jill wasn't gone after the Lavinia incident, it certainly now. I have ensured this through my actions in Los Angeles and Lausanne.

Separations are chaotic and difficult even in the best of circumstances, but they are far more problematic here. I'm less than a month into a year-long tour. It's not an option to cancel a leg, or even reschedule a run of shows, so that I can return to the United Kingdom and deal with the legal and logistical fallout from my divorce. This is not comforting to my wife—in fact, it aggravates the situation—but I have a slew of professional duties on my plate and must consider the broader picture. These are massive concerts that employ dozens and dozens of people and entertain hundreds of thousands of fans worldwide. The juggernaut must continue on.

Two weeks after Paris, mid-May 1994, I am on the other side of the Atlantic. I'll begin the North American part with four nights at Mexico's Palacio de los Deportes, a spectacular, 26,000-capacity circular dome built for the 1968 Olympics. It's an incredible place to start a hectic three-month tour. I've never played Mexico before, alone or with Genesis, so there's a lot of anticipation. The concerts have become a national event. For 100,000 Mexican fans—some of the world's most fervent music fans—I have to keep one set of emotions under control while fully expressing another. I have let down my family. I don't want to let down the supporters either.

The Both Sides of the World tour continues, as it must. My schedule is frequently up in the air, and we're now dealing with complex and ever-changing time discrepancies between the United States and the United Kingdom. So there are only a few occasions when I can sit down in peace and quiet and make those painful phone calls home. I want to speak with Jill and Lily. I also want to speak with Simon and

Joely and explain the issue to them, but it would require going via Andy, which is a whole other universe of anguish.

However, on the rare occasions when I am able to call Jill, I have difficulty getting through. Nonetheless, Jill periodically joins me on tour in the United States—Lily wants to see me. Bless her, she's trying to push through it all and, in her young heart, believes that whatever is wrong will soon be fixed. On more than one occasion, I'll be standing center stage, singing "Separate Lives," which is undoubtedly a really emotional moment in the musical. And everytime Jill is in the crowd, she goes down the side aisle and stands beside the stage, staring at me.

Three weeks into the North American leg, six weeks after Paris, I handwrite a four- or five-page letter in which I try to express how I feel about us and the future. The most dependable and efficient way to deliver this letter to her is to fax it rather than mail it. So, it is what I do. But it does not help. Things remain complex and convoluted, with communication channels still disrupted.

We're here in Frankfurt, playing three nights at the 100-year-old Festhalle. I've been in one area for 72 hours, and there's just one hour's time difference between Germany and Britain. So I figure this is a good time to meet up with Jill and iron out a few things. But I can't do it. I can never seem to get through. Thinking I had no other choice, I fax her again at Lakers Lodge.

All hell has broken loose. The fax I sent from my dressing room in Frankfurt has somehow made its way into Britain's best-selling tabloid. The Sun's editing and usage of what I actually wrote resulted in the headline "I'M FAXING FURIOUS," and the report that I was faxing for divorce.

All hell breaks loose. The press gathers outside Orianne's parents' house. Her father is dying of cancer, which is the last thing they need. Reporters approached my mother, brother, and sister. Anyone who knows me is contacted for opinion, and the story becomes a national hot topic. Actually, scratch that—it's a worldwide talking topic. I've learned not to enter a hotel through the front door for fear of being ambushed by the paparazzi.

This scrutiny is difficult for me to bear, especially because the crux of the story is false. For Orianne, a twenty-one-year-old suddenly immersed in a world she knows nothing about, it is horrific. She has to look behind herself wherever she walks.

The timing of "Faxgate" is so perfect that it's terrible. I've been hired to do an MTV Unplugged event at Wembley TV Studios in London to promote the tour's U.K. leg. I'm contractually obligated; else, this would be the last thing I'd do right now. Walking onstage in Birmingham a few days later, I still think this is the worst conceivable time to begin a tour at home. I've gone from Mr. Really, Really Nice Guy (though a little ubiquitous and annoying) to Mr. Bastard.

As I previously stated, the play begins with debris on the floor: corrugated iron, bins, and scrunched-up newspapers. The first song, "I Don't Care Anymore," from the Hello, I Must Be Going! album, is performed as a drum duet with Ricky. That song was composed about my first failed marriage while Andy and I were going through the legal process. As a result, the lyrics are caustic, and I play it in a moody manner, scuffing my way through the debris placed on stage.

However, everything is now more resonant. The lyrics have nothing to do with Jill or my marriage. However, when I kick those newspapers, it appears like I am also kicking the tabloids.

After the opening song, I sit on the stage at Birmingham's NEC and tell the audience, "Listen, this is all very embarrassing, but you mustn't believe everything you read in the papers..." I'm not sure if that puts anyone at ease, perhaps not even me. I was constantly advised in the theater, "Never apologize to the audience." Simply get on with it." But I imagine there was a small sigh of relief. "Thank God we got that out of the way."

Introducing "I Wish It Would Rain Down," from... But seriously, I perform my version of a skit by politically incorrect, angry (and incredibly humorous) comedian Sam Kinison (a buddy who died two years ago). It's about a couple in a car bickering about their husband's previous girlfriend, whom they've recently seen. My thoughts: it's me, doing some acting, talking about my love of comedians, then segueing into a song in a characterful manner. In my ignorance, I don't think this is too close to the bone for some. That it would appear that I'm dancing on the grave of my marriage. I'm just trying to make the audience laugh or relieve the stress that I sense is there. To my embarrassment, I don't understand why it's in terrible taste given the circumstances.

The 1994 European leg concludes with eight nights at Wembley Arena. Sounds impressive, and on many levels it is. However, a London crowd is unlike any other; even at the best of times, there will be a sense of "so impress me". But now, every night, there is a segment of the audience who considers me a villain.

Orianne joins me whenever she can schedule a few days off from Capital Ventures. She arrives in, seemingly immune to jet lag, and we spend the entire night talking and catching up. These are fleeting moments, hours of happiness in the midst of a thirteen-month global tour and a disintegrating marriage.

There are no winners in this scenario. I am lucky enough to be able to immerse myself in my profession. Unfortunately, my job requires me to be in the spotlight, in front of thousands of people who are reading all about my miserable private life.

Night after night, staring beyond the stage lights, I don't see the tens of thousands of people having a good time. I see the strange huddle that is holding heated conversations: "I used to like him. But now he's abandoned his wife for this young girlfriend, a bimbo who he's attempting to shape into what he wants. But he's not taking our money for nothing; we're still going to the concert! Let's see how far he has fallen! Oh, I enjoy this song. What a jerk, though. This is also an excellent one, however it pertains to his first marriage. Another ex! Can't Phil Collins straighten himself out via fax?"

Now I'm not sure where I am. I feel as if I have lost control. My human standing—my dignity, or lack thereof—is being buffeted by events that have been reduced to newspaper headlines. The cumulative consequence is that I want to write myself off the script. I want to wipe the chalkboard clear and declare, "I don't want any part of this. Because it is now too much. "I have too much baggage."

That wound festers and worsens.

Despite the personal upheaval, I do not consider the album to be a negative experience. It was incredibly enjoyable to make. Writing, playing, and recording all on my own was extremely liberating. That is why I choose to liberate myself in different ways. During the marketing of Both Sides—before the tour, before Orianne—I inform Tony Smith that I am leaving Genesis.

Chapter 15: Taxgate

Should I stay or go? Do I leave Jill, Genesis, or the United Kingdom? The three years between reconnecting with Lavinia in summer 1992 during Genesis' We Can't Dance tour and ending my Both Sides of the World tour in spring 1995 were more than a bit turbulent. The Imperial Eighties have evolved into the Emotional Nineties. Which decade thrilled me the most, and which threw me off the most? Even now, it's difficult to say.

Thinking back to the We Can't Dance tour, I understand that the pressure of leading the band finally got to me. From the commencement of Genesis' biggest-ever global tour, there was a sense of nostalgia and "look how far we've come." This was most evident in the material we presented on the screens during "I Know What I Like": a lot of vintage film dating back to the Peter era. It was moving objects. However, there were several issues and niggles right away.

After opening night at Texas Stadium in Irving, Texas, we travel via Houston to Florida. I acquire a sore throat and seek acupuncture backstage at Miami's Joe Robbie Stadium. The next night, in Tampa, I only get through one song, "Land of Confusion," before apologizing and departing stage left, my singing voice in tatters. So much for acupuncture. Half the stadium is chanting "awwwwww" in sympathy. The other 20,000 yell something like "Bastard!" "I paid my money; sing the songs!" I scurry back into the changing room and cry. It's simply too intense. I've let everyone down, including fans, crew, caterers, and the entire team that works in and around the stadium. It's a hefty responsibility and a difficult time. It's entirely on me. In my perspective, I've already ruined Genesis' biggest-ever tour after only one week.

But, as I am accustomed to doing, I soldier on, and the tour continues. As we tick off the world's enormodomes and super-stadiums, a question arises: do I truly want this, this pressure, this obligation? Can I sustain this—the singing, the banter, the larger-than-life performances—through a tough summer schedule, all the way to an eye-wateringly massive outdoor homecoming show at Knebworth?

A tour of this extent reflects Genesis' astonishing success in the early 1990s. However, having to do it is a huge pain in the arse.

And what happens next? What happens on the tour following the stadium and arena tours? After four nights at Wembley and six nights at Earls Court, what is the next aim, the next height? Anything less indicates that we have peaked. Anything more would leave us exhausted.

Plus, for the majority of the tour, I'll have to impress those crowds while maintaining a brave face for the Jumbotrons. If there is such a thing as cardiac vertigo, I have it bad.

That is the mentality I bring to the writing and recording of Both Sides. All along, Tony Smith has been walking glass. He is one of the few who knows what happened to Lavinia. He is also aware that, as a result, Jill and I are on very dangerous ground. He understands that my current mental state has resulted in this fairly dismal solo album, and that cheerful eighties pop sensation Phil Collins is dying on the inside.

Tony, the ever-observant boss and confidant, is right to be concerned, but not about my personal life.

In late 1993, Tony and I are on a private plane flying to fulfill some album promotion duties. We are the only two people on board, sitting together at a table near the back of the plane. I haven't told anyone about my future plans, although I've already decided. I adore promoting Both Sides through media interviews. This, in my opinion, is my finest hour, a highly personal album full of songs with something to talk about.

In late 1993, I was traveling to promote Both Sides, and my life was very chaotic. I've created what I believe to be my best record, but at what cost? The idea came from the perspiration of trying to figure out where my brain and heart were. These are songs about separation and love lost. Furthermore, the flexibility with which I created them fills me with anticipation. What if I make more records like Both Sides, which are individualistic and self-sufficient? Why should I make more band albums?

In conclusion, for both positive and negative reasons, it is time for me to quit Genesis after dedicating half of my life to the band. I simply cannot tell anyone about it.

So I keep quiet for more than two years, returning to earth with a jolt. Terra infirma. In Switzerland. Now it is time to address the women in my life.

Those around me, I sense, believe I'm insane. Tony Smith, in particular, understands that leaving Genesis and my second marriage will cost me terribly, twice over and in every way. I do not care. I need to get out.

I don't blame Genesis for the ongoing trauma in my own life. Perhaps I felt obligated to agree to tours, schedules, and projects to keep everyone happy and employed. But, ultimately, the buck stops with me. I could have declined that follow-up album, that final tour of America, and the most recent offer to produce. And I could have said no to Orianne—or rather, not pursued her with such zeal.

During the Both Sides tour, I determine that after I'm done, I'll go live with her in Switzerland. To a man who has been chastised in the British press, boltholes don't get much safer or more hospitable than the little, mountain-and-lake-ringed, democracy-loving country where discretion is one of the most valuable natural resources. There are few places cleaner than Switzerland for me to get away from all my adult interactions, both personal and professional.

That's how others may perceive my thoughts.

It's just that Orianne lives in Switzerland. So I went where she lives. The "only" thing I'm guilty of is being a married 44-year-old man who has fallen in love.

In a few interviews, I've attempted to convey this. I told a UK journalist that if Orianne lived in Grimsby or Hull, I would have gone. The tabloid soon searches out residents of Grimsby and Hull for their thoughts on my statements, implying that The Faxing Tax Exile is now laying into genuine English burghers. Another wave of unfavorable publicity, followed by a bombardment of nasty emails from Grimsby and Hull asking, "What's the matter with our towns?"

Still, the fortuitous advantage of going to Switzerland is that people tend to keep to themselves and leave you alone. If they don't, you have the legal right to shoot anyone entering your yard. Right now, something about it appeals.

Switzerland makes me very pleased right away. While I certainly have a massive self-made mess to clean up, life on the ground quickly simplifies.

Every day in Geneva, I visit a local bar while waiting for Orianne to finish her work. The bartender says to me, "Why do you want to live here? We are all attempting to get out." They want out for the same reasons that I want in. The natural beauty, the sluggish pace, and the deafening stillness are all happiness to me. After twenty-five years as public property, I now get to be private property. It took some harsh measures, but I've written myself out of the story.

Our first home is on the southern side of Lake Geneva, in a rented townhouse in the ancient village of Hermance, near the French border. There are four floors, one room each floor, and no straight walls. It's beautiful, a little skew-whiff heaven.

In Switzerland, life is more family-oriented, in a loving, old-fashioned sense. Orianne's father had cancer when I met her, and he died tragically the night I performed in Stuttgart as part of the Both Sides Tour. I had flown to Orianne shortly following the show.

With Mum and Dad splitting up, Dad dying in 1972, and me spending the next twenty-odd years on the road, I've lost the sense of being part of a larger family for nearly a quarter of a century, or virtually my entire adulthood. Andy's family was in Vancouver, while Jill's was in Los Angeles. In Switzerland, everyone is together. This is something comfy and familiar, yet it has nothing to do with who I am or what I do.

What about the rest of my family? It's complicated, to say the least.

It's quite difficult for Jill to deal with this situation. One of the first things she says when I tell her I'm moving to Switzerland is, "You don't speak French!" She is correct, but it does not matter to me. I can and do learn.

I try to see Lily, who is now six, as often as possible. I fly back to the UK and stay at dreadful Holiday Inns or airport hotels. I pick her up from school, and we sit in the car, talking or listening to the music to the latest Disney film, Aladdin, on repeat, while we wait for the Italian restaurant in Cranleigh, Surrey to open. A challenging and terrible situation for all involved.

The first time Orianne sees Lily is in Ascot—I can't stay in London since the press is still behind me, so I choose a modest rural hotel near Tittenhurst Park, the former Lennon mansion I rented with Brand X.

Orianne does not see Simon or Joely for a while. Baby steps. Inheriting a family may be painful for everyone involved. But Orianne, a bright, clever woman, takes everything with stride.

We begin looking for a proper, family-friendly home to live, keeping in mind that I need to finalize things—I want my kids to be able to come visit as soon as possible. However, the Swiss are wary of such things. A foreigner cannot simply arrive in their nation and purchase a large family home. They must first obtain what is known as a C permit. To obtain a C permit, you must demonstrate a commitment to staying in Switzerland by holding a B visa for five years, demonstrating that you are not simply swooping in and purchasing a house as a tax-free vacation hideaway.

It takes a while, but we eventually find the perfect home. Begnins, a little village midway between Geneva and Lausanne, is surrounded by vineyards. Clayton House is a 7,000-square-foot estate that includes seven bedrooms, six bathrooms, a tennis court, pool, pool house and stunning views of Lake Geneva and the Alps. Unfortunately, Sir Jackie Stewart, a motor racing great already owns it.

Luckily, Sir Jackie is a friend, and he and his wife Helen are eager to return to the United Kingdom. We rent the house from Jackie for a while, but after I've convinced the Swiss authorities of my good intentions and dedication to their beautiful country, I purchase Clayton House.

I feel settled, stable, and substantial. This is the first time...ever.

I'm not sure if word of my newfound independence has spread, but I later discover that in January 1996, my name is spreading in an unusual new context. A Doctor Who television movie is in the works, and I, along with Scott Glenn and Randy Quaid, am being considered to play the Time Lord's arch-rival, the Master. Finally, scheduling precludes me from being formally contacted to portray the cosmic baddie, which is probably a good thing. I can't really compare touring with a band to traveling through space and time.

It's obvious we can no longer ignore the Genesis news. I want to "out" myself as a previous frontman, and Mike and Tony need to be able to move forward with whatever they have planned next.

I fly to London to meet Tony Smith at his place. I believe our manager informed Tony and Mike of my goals long ago. But I'm still nervous. These are my oldest musical buddies. Two of my oldest buddies, period. And I am going to properly say farewell to them.

Secretly, I'm overjoyed that they're making preparations to continue. I don't want the band to break up, and I certainly don't want to be responsible for it. I simply want escape.

We hug, wish each other well, and then say our goodbyes. We know we'll see each other again, just not in the same light.

Our management issues a news statement on March 28, 1996, making the following official announcement: "Genesis ends 20-year experiment and replaces Peter Gabriel as vocalist..." For the past 20 years, drummer Phil Collins has temped as singer, to great acclaim.

Chapter 16: Goodbye to All That

What do you call someone who hangs out with musicians? A drummer.

Have you heard about the drummer who graduated high school? I am neither.

What was the last thing a drummer said in a band? "Hey, guys, how about we try one of my songs?"

It is not simple to be a drummer. I've heard every joke. I understand that it takes five of us to change a lightbulb—one to screw it in, four to discuss how much better Steve Gadd would have done it. I've yucked along to the one about the drummer who died, got to heaven, and was surprised to hear some fantastic drumming coming from behind the Pearly Gates, prompting him to rush to St. Peter to inquire if that was Buddy Rich performing. "No, that is God. He just thinks he is Buddy Rich. I should have shared that with Tony Bennett.

I get accustomed to the fractures early on. Drummers need to grow robust skin, particularly on our fingertips. We're the most physical guys on stage, and we need to keep up. After the show, the drummer is exhausted, covered in perspiration and panting in the dressing room. I do not mind. That's our role. Keeping the beat and feeling it.

By the time I finished the highly physical A Trip into the Light tour—a hectic, in-the-round play—in 1997 and marshalled the troops for the second Big Band tour in 1998, I'd had the show on the road for over thirty years. Although I have long ago delegated the hard lifting of drumming to either Chester Thompson or Ricky Lawson, both outstanding drummers, I still keep my hand in, ensuring that at some time during every gig on every tour, I play drums sufficiently to keep my chops sharp. I always return to the comforting embrace of the drum stool. She's my first love and the source of all my power.

In terms of pure physical strength, I have rarely faltered during my three decades of performance. Blisters are about as unpleasant as it gets. After any amount of time at home, you'd have softened up. After a few weeks of bathing the kids or cleaning up after dinner, your dishwashing hands will feel as soft as your face. You'd suddenly have to go on tour again, and your fingers would need to be gig-ready and hardened.

Some, like The Police's Stewart Copeland, wear gloves. I could never do that. I need to feel the stick.

So there's no way around it. You simply need to acquire strength and resilience. On early tours, in my hotel room, I'd play on pillows in front of the TV all night to strengthen my wrists. You must persevere despite the blisters. When the blister bursts, you get a blood blister, which breaks and you're left with increasingly mangled flesh.

You have no choice but to do it raw, in real time, onstage. Even if you rehearsed for seven, eight, nine, or ten hours a day, you will not get there. You will not experience the stress, anxieties, or strain that comes with performing in a show. So the fingers will not be hardened either. You might apply New-Skin, which is similar to a thick nail varnish and is applied to a portion of flayed epidermis in severe need of protection. You paint it, and it stings and stinks. But as it dries, the terrible medical pong and discomfort go, and you're left with another layer of insulation. When that falls off, it pulls away another layer of genuine flesh. You begin all over again.

While all this may sound dramatic, drummers must deal with it on a daily basis. You play on and on. In desperation, you may apply plasters, but the sweat will cause them to fall off during the show, so you hope to build hard skin. Otherwise, the salty sweat will make your cracked, bleeding digits feel like they're on fire.

The voice, however, is a distinct animal. You can't apply a sticking plaster on strained vocal cords. So you must try to transcend through other means.

Fortunately, I never had nodules on any of the large Genesis or solo tours in the 1980s or 1990s. There was a doctor in every port. I rarely canceled gigs because I knew when to pull the emergency wire and get an injection of prednisone, a corticosteroid.

Your vocal chords are really little, like two tiny coins that rub together. If they get swollen or mistreated, they will not come together to allow you to sing a note. Then you are in trouble. If you continue to abuse them, their engorged state will eventually turn into nodules. However, a brief steroid shot decreases the swelling, and you're good as rain. In the short run, anyway.

So you get an injection of prednisone injected into your bum. The steroid will get you through the show, but once you take it, you'll be on it for ten days. It will also cause a slew of adverse effects, including erratic mood swings, water retention, and moon face.

This occurred in Fremantle, Australia, during the massive Invisible Touch tour in 1986 and 1987. Touring Australia is a massive undertaking—different time zones, hefty internal flights, upside down and back to front at the bottom of the world.

This is the tour that we run into Elton John. Ray Cooper, my old percussionist friend, is a member of his band. We went to watch him because we're playing at the same place shortly after. Ray asks, "Hey, man, have you been working out?" Of course I have not. He hurriedly adds, "You look great, you look great…" with a hint of protest.

When I return to the hotel, I examine myself in the mirror. "I look OK," I believe, at least to myself.

Those pictures terrified me. I had disregarded the warning: "Do not operate heavy machinery while under the influence." And the apparatus does not get much heavier than a Genesis stadium tour.

When I met Ray a short time later, during a gig at the Royal Albert Hall, he admitted that the only "working out" he was doing in Australia was figuring out why his old friend Phil looked so "fucking terrible."

And it wasn't just the tour. As previously discussed, the eye-wateringly long and climactic My voice broke in Tampa, virtually derailing the We Can't Dance tour from the beginning. The audience on this trip was massive, and they knew the lines better than I did. I could not let them down. However, even the needle couldn't salvage the show that night.

By this point, I'd been dancing about the high notes for quite some time. This did not happen as frequently on my solo tours because my music was written specifically for me to sing. However, some of the

144

Genesis songs were composed specifically for Peter's voice. Despite our amazing vocal similarities, some songs were simply above my ability. Even if Peter had been singing them, they would have been too high for him at this time in our lives.

Certain songs on the Genesis setlist made me fear what was coming next. "Home by the Sea" contains numerous lyrics. I had to recall the beginnings of the lines as a crucial aide-mémoire. Tony Banks wrote the tune and the lyrics, but he had never considered how it would sound; he had never performed it out loud. To get through the show, I had to carefully thread my way around some of the accident black patches.

Finally, there's "In the Air Tonight." If I sang so coldly, it would be difficult to reach the emotional peaks that drive the song. Sometimes your body movements and mouth form might help you get there. However, if I were drumming as well, the distraction would catapult my voice to new heights. In this way, one assisted the other: the drumming propelled the singing.

Mostly, though, I didn't give myself much time to think about these issues. For three decades, I pressed. What's disturbing is that if I tallied how many times I've been stabbed in the buttocks for a good singing performance, I'd have difficulty sitting down. I'd have problems getting back up, too: as I'd later discover, too much cortisone can make your bones brittle.

In 1998, the Tarzan experience is coming to an end, and we need to record a "pop" version of "You'll Be in My Heart" for the single release.

One afternoon in Ocean Way, we are listening back to a voice take. I'm in the voice booth, wearing headphones, when the engineer clicks play.

Bang!

It's extremely loud. That is incredible. Forget ear-splitting; this is head-splitting. The sound from the headphones rushes directly into me, overwhelming and explosive. I became deaf in one ear. As simple and quick as that. I hear nothing in my left ear. There was no ringing or buzzing, just nothing.

I politely tell the engineer, "Please don't do that again."

I return to my hotel, the Peninsula Beverly Hills, rather bewildered. Lily, now nine, is waiting for me, which brightens things up considerably. She and I start playing Spyro the Dragon; computer games are one of our new common interests. I adore them and Spyro, but if it comes to it, I'll declare myself a Crash Bandicoot fan. My left ear's hearing returns almost instantly. It's as if I've been underwater, but the barrier has suddenly vanished. Thank God for it.

That evening, we head out to eat at a little Italian restaurant beside the hotel. I'm going to eat my pasta when my hearing suddenly fails again. Since then, I've been unable to hear well in my left ear. The game is done, just like that.

I discover that a virus has damaged the cells in the nerves that connect my brain to my ear. This has resulted in the loss of my capacity to hear intermediate and low frequencies. It could have been different if I had dealt with it right away—with a dosage of my old friend cortisone, which has the potential to jumpstart cell regeneration. However, as is typical of Collins, I left it too late. My father's failure to manage his diabetes and heart disease was ultimately fatal.

Because this is a viral infection, the noise in the headphones was likely not the cause. However, as the months and years pass, it's the only unusual hearing experience I've had, so I can't help but think it's partly to blame.

I am not completely deaf, only 50% in one ear, so I can continue working from home. It could be an issue if I was performing with a rock band or leading my own band in a large pop spectacle. But I don't intend to do either for the foreseeable future.

I'm content here, nestled in my garden on a Swiss mountainside. I write music for films. I have a Big Band that only plays in smaller settings and for whom I rarely sing. I have all the time in the world to make my next solo album. So, if I have to cease being the "Phil

Collins" of headlines and headline-act (dis)repute, I am fine with that. My get-out clause is partially responsible for my hearing loss.

I'm upbeat about this new, semi-deaf existence, which is perplexing to my loved ones. But the truth is that losing my hearing has given me control. It is disability-induced control, but I will accept it. After years of paying the piper but not fully calling the song, I can reclaim my destiny.

I've grown to despise this "Phil Collins" doppelgänger, who was out there performing, flaunting himself, collecting compliments and (increasingly) criticism. "Phil Collins" carries aggravations, expectancies, duties, and suppositions around his ankles and hanging over his neck. He has fractured households, hostile partners, and estranged children. I do not like that person. I do not want to be that guy. I've had enough of myself.

Brother Bear's creation is yet another lengthy creative process, as one could anticipate from a narrative with a King Lear undertone in its original form.

Primarily, Disney's music team insists that I get a computer. Before this, I was dealing with tape. On Tarzan, every time they made changes to the film, the songs were affected, so I had to go away and re-record everything. It took a long time, but I had no choice. With computers, you may change the tempo and music at will.

I take a week-long course with Chuck Choi, one of Mark Mancina's technical wizards. I take copious notes, and at first glance, it appears to be a daunting task. But before long, I'd developed an interest in computers. I've created my own new ways of working in a studio, and I'm sitting elbow to elbow with guys who live and breathe this stuff. Mark is a seasoned scorewriter, youthful and eager, and a die-hard Genesis fan. We get along well, we split the music cues to be completed, and I get to work—a very eager, soundtrack-composing, Disney-affiliated, partially deaf man.

Even more back-and-forth when Mark tries to transform my underscoring into a proper orchestral chart. We learn that pieces I wrote for a flute are out of the flute's range, or that my trombone part is actually a French horn piece. I'm quickly discovering that, despite my extensive musical background, when it comes to film scoring, I don't know my oboe from my arse.

We enlisted Richie Havens, a longstanding hero of mine, to write the song "Great Spirits," which opens the film. He makes a lovely version, but it isn't enough for the squad. After several more tryouts, we decide to contact Tina Turner. However, she has recently declared her retirement, making it difficult to get her services. Fortunately, I met her with Eric while filming August—she collaborated with him on "Tearing Us Apart." She also resides in Switzerland, which is another plus for Collins, who stays home.

Tina says yes, so we head to Zurich to record her. She learned the song from the tape I supplied her, demonstrating her professionalism and artistry. She gives it her best, and after a few takes, we've got it. Tina exudes melody and class.

Another powerful tune, "Transformation," serves as the soundtrack for the film's man-to-bear transition. My lyrics are translated into Inuit and performed by the Bulgarian Women's Choir. On paper, this appears to be an odd juxtaposition and a surprising choice. The end film is outstanding.

I do end up singing six of the songs as bonus tracks on the soundtrack album, so I'm partially satisfied. However, it is thought appropriate to have The Blind Boys of Alabama perform "Welcome," one of my best songs for the film. It's for a hunting scene in which the bear clan welcomes the hero bear into the larger ursine family through an orgy of salmon fishing. The salmon appear weirdly unconcerned.

Still, when Brother Bear premieres in October 2003 at Broadway's New Amsterdam Theatre, I'll get the opportunity to share the stage alongside Tina Turner. Following the movie, I perform one of my songs, "No Way Out," before introducing Tina, who performs "Great Spirits" with me on drums. It's amazing how Tina turns it on. She'll stroll through the soundcheck, "pretend" she's retired, and then crush the song and provide a flawless performance.

In addition to Brother Bear, I've been gently working on songs for my seventh solo album from home.

In late summer 2000, we learn that Orianne is pregnant. Nicholas Grev Austin Collins was born on April 21, 2001, with "Grev" honoring my father and "Austin" honoring my brother Clive (it's his middle name) and paternal grandfather. This lovely period prompts a fresh crop of writing. "Come with Me" is about Nic as a baby, but it applies to any baby. It's a surge of pure paternal love and care: don't worry about anything, just come with me and close your eyes; everything will be fine.

The lyrics apply to any of my children, or any children wherever. It's one of my favorite songs, and the tune reminds me of a lullaby I used to sing to Lily in the back of limos in America. We create a music box for baby Nic to help him sleep and play that song. I'll then have to write one for his brother Matt and purchase his own music box. Much to his dismay, at the time of writing, his melody had yet to be transformed into a song.

I decided to label this extremely personal new album Testify, which sums exactly how I felt about my life at the moment. I want to tell the world about a woman I adore and our new baby child. I'm enjoying my time underground in Switzerland right now.

It will thus take something spectacular to bring me, blinking, back to the center of the stage. The extraordinary thing is a call from Her Majesty.

In spring 2002, I was asked to be the drummer for the house band for the Party at the Palace, a sumptuous event hosted at Buckingham Palace to commemorate Queen Elizabeth II's Golden Jubilee. I can't turn that down, questionable ear or not.

Come performance day, my hands hold up, my ear doesn't bother me, and everyone is in top form—including Brian May, who is performing on the roof of Buckingham Palace in wind that must be a nightmare for his sound, not to mention his hair.

Five months later, Testify is released. I'm here to tell you it fails miserably. The French, Swiss, Swedes, Germans, Dutch, and

Belgians, bless 'em all, show it some love by placing it at number 2, 3, or 4 on their national charts. But the rest of the free world, especially United Kingdom. and the United States, are less enthusiastic.

I will also testify before you that I am genuinely philosophical about this. I had over 15 minutes.

On the plus side, I've created an album that celebrates my love for my wife and baby child, largely at home, and while dealing with abrupt deafness that appeared to have ended everything. That must be counted as a result.

Another important component in my decision-making process. Three years after my abrupt deafness, life is nearly normal. My brain has adjusted, my right ear has compensated, and my hearing impairments have leveled off. I can again listen to and enjoy music. And, as I discovered at Queen Liz's small gig, wearing in-ear monitors makes performing much easier.

I'm completely unaware of anything going on as I prepare for the tour in early 2004. My mind is very much elsewhere. But I return to domestic life in the spring, when Orianne informs me that she is pregnant again. Fantastic news. For the first time in my life, I embrace the concept of paternity leave: the tour schedule is quickly rerouted to ensure that we will be at home for the birth and for some time thereafter.

The first Final Farewell tour begins on June 1, 2004, at Milan's Fila Forum. We'll be touring Europe and America until the end of September, when I'll say goodbye to the States at the Office Depot Center in Fort Lauderdale.

Before I depart America, I take advantage of a day off following the Houston event. Knowing that my retirement is approaching—and that this could be my final trip to Texas—I make a special pilgrimage to San Antonio, home of the Alamo.

It's been 50 years since I first saw the Disney picture Davy Crockett: King of the Wild Frontier on television as a five-year-old, which piqued my curiosity in the struggle between 185 Texans and a few thousand Mexican troops. However, what began as childhood games with toy troops and a fort in the lawn at 453 Hanworth Road has evolved into a serious adult passion.

In 1973, during Genesis' Foxtrot tour, I took Peter Gabriel to the historic location to investigate the truth behind the Hollywood myth. It was fantastic and poignant to see the Alamo's renowned church façade firsthand; to me, the site of the brutal thirteen-day siege was sacred ground. I couldn't wait to return, and on a future trip to the city, I encountered a clairvoyant who claimed that in a past incarnation, I was one of the 185 defenders—a courier named John W. Smith. I would have taken it with a pinch of gunpowder if it hadn't been for the fact that I used to end my boyhood games by lighting fire to my toy soldiers—which, I subsequently discovered, was the Texans' fate.

On a day off from another tour of the United States in Washington, D.C., maybe in the mid-1980s, I wound up in a shop called The Gallery of History. It offered historical papers, and among its collection of Nazi military orders and signed Beethoven scores, I discovered a letter penned by Davy Crockett. It was priced at $60,000. Crockett was my hero, but I couldn't rationalize paying so much for a piece of paper, no matter how wonderful it was to feel so close to the famed frontiersman.

But I was intrigued and began quietly hunting for other battle-related items, though it wasn't until Christmas 1995 that I received my first Alamo document, a present from Orianne: a receipt for a saddle owned by the aforementioned courier Smith. He was out delivering final letters when the Alamo fell on March 6, 1836, and I couldn't help thinking about how far that saddle had traveled in the name of Texas. Since then, I've been a collector of all things Alamo, purchasing weapons and documents whenever chance and budget allowed—and occasionally when they didn't.

Now, thinking that 2004 will be my last tour of America, I hire a tiny plane to return to the spot. I bring Orianne, a three-year-old Nicholas, and Danny Gillen with me. As I leave the Alamo following a ninety-minute private tour, I see a store twenty yards from the compound's northeast corner, which has seen some of the worst bloodshed.

Inside The History Shop, I talk to manager Jim Guimarin. It's the start of a wonderful friendship and fruitful relationship—Jim will assist me with my collecting ambitions in the future years.

After the American leg of The First Final Farewell Tour, I return home for two months. Mathew Thomas Clemence Collins is born on December 1, 2004, in Geneva. I'm a very happy father all over again. All of my older children appear to be as content as I am, and I am finally on the point of giving up the touring life of a musician in order to become a stay-at-home dad and help raise the kids.

I am off work until October 2005, when we continue the final leg of the tour at the Saku Suurhall in Tallinn, Estonia. The shows are great. The last stretch is really impressive, not least because I'm performing in areas like Estonia, Lithuania, and Finland that I've never visited before. My hearing is also fine, which is a great comfort. Everyone is having a blast. Could I retire at my age (I'll be fifty-four at the end of the tour)?

But my determination to stop is unshakable. I said that would be the end. I have to keep my word. I need to go home. If nothing else, it's only fair that while I'm saying my final goodbyes, Orianne is stranded at home, either pregnant while mothering a toddler or, in the second leg, nursing a baby while mothering a toddler. With an absent husband, she has a lot on her plate.

I'm counting down the days until I can get off the road, put an end to a lifetime of performance, go home, and settle into a profession I've always wanted but never had the opportunity to enjoy: that of a Proper Dad. A full-time father. On both previous occasions, with Simon and Joely, and then with Lily, I hadn't even managed to be a nine-to-five parent. We have all paid the price for that. This time, with my two infant sons, I will do right by them. I have a lot of love to give and, of course, a lot of making up to do. It is family time.

Orianne is simultaneously thinking and concerned. She is confident that my retirement will be complete, with no working for me or anyone else.

But Orianne has no desire to give up her work, become a full-time mother, or settle down as a full-time companion to a disconnected and indolent retiree. She is creative, with a master's degree in International Management and a bachelor's degree in Commerce, and has ran her own business, O-com, which organizes events.

Her dynamism was one of the driving elements behind a charity that we founded in 2000. For years, I'd been getting letters from teenagers asking for guidance on how to break into the music business, and other than providing them a few connections, I didn't know what else to say. Orianne and I discussed this at home one night and devised a plan to establish a foundation that would provide tuition, coaching, and assistance in the disciplines of music, the arts, and sports. We approached our acquaintances in these disciplines and requested them to be godparents in their respective fields of competence. This is how the Little Dreams Foundation started.

If you're unhappy at home, touring can be the hardest place to maintain a positive attitude. Still, by the time I resume the final two-month run in October 2005, a part of me is happy for the distraction. Perhaps some distance will benefit both of us. I can take more time to consider our future and Orianne's requirements. She has the ability to take her time recovering, even if she is caring for two young children.

However, on the few occasions when she comes to meet me on tour, things remain strained. We are bickering during our downtime in motels. During the band van's journeys to the airport, the silences are chilly and awkward, exacerbated by the uneasiness of the other members of the touring group. Joely, who has accompanied me on the tour, is particularly sensitive of the disharmony. The festive gleam of this First Final Farewell tour is fading. The paradise of our marriage and our young family is fading.

There is undoubtcdly a profound love, but Orianne and I are currently unable to uncover it.

I can't stop thinking, "I don't believe this. Here I go again. Again, I am on tour, and my marriage is rough, if not worse. Third time unlucky. And what is the common denominator? Me. No one can be blamed.

If I were to sum up what's driving the breakup between Orianne and me, I'd say it's my responsibility for not hearing her cry out. I don't understand why we're battling and why I'm being forced out of the marital bed. I just don't understand it. I apologize.

Nic is four and a half, and Matt is not even one. If things go as I expect, my children will be taken from me. They've got no idea. The sensation of déjà vu makes me ill to my stomach.

When The First Final Farewell tour concludes on November 24, 2005, at Prague's Sazka Arena, Orianne and I will still be together in the sense that we are still married, at least on paper. We're still living in the same house, but not for long.

What do you call a drummer who has split up with his girlfriend? Homeless.

What do you call a drummer who has split up with his third wife? A mess.

Chapter 17: Turn It On Again, Turn It Off Again

The last six weeks of 2005 offer a traffic gridlock of competing demands. Actually, it's more of a vehicle wreck. The following impact causes more than just fenders to bend out of shape.

In mid-November, the five core members of Genesis will meet in Glasgow, the latest destination on my First Final Farewell tour, to explore a much-anticipated reunion.

At the end of November, the tour comes to a close, and I return home to a home that no longer feels like mine, and a young family in desperate need of emergency care.

In December, Disney urgently requests my presence on Broadway to begin production on a theatrical musical adaptation of Tarzan—four months earlier than planned, and on the day after Christmas.

In summary, my work-life balance is once again completely out of whack. So much for retiring.

Live, the Lamb never got a fair shake of the tail. Personally, I feel like I didn't say goodbye to Genesis properly, and neither did we to our fans. After twelve years apart, I miss Mike and Tony. Equally, it would be fantastic to get back behind the kit and simply drum with the band. Furthermore, an ambitious, expensive, multimedia theatrical production of The Lamb would not lend itself to a lengthy tour of the world's largest venues. This would be shorter and far more artistic than the original trip. It would be limited to a few nights in a nice theater, perhaps even on Broadway, with the rest of the world's interest satisfied by a live online stream or cinema broadcast. The possibilities are thrilling.

So, for the first time in thirty years, all five of us sat down together. Tony Smith and Mike Large, Peter's manager, were also present.

The environment is pleasant. We're there to discuss details and set firm rehearsal and performance dates, assuming Peter can decide whether or not to participate. With him, it's "go." Without him, there is "no point."

It quickly becomes apparent that playing The Lamb Set with today's technology—that is, with today's technology functioning properly—will necessitate a significant amount of time, effort, and passion from everyone. Without saying anything, we all know this indicates a truce between Peter and Tony. The feasibility of this entire operation will depend on who holds the reins and directs traffic. The possibilities are limitless, but as industrial technology evolves and new pathways emerge, so do the risks.

Similarly, we all know that there can be no disagreements on ideas, but Peter will want to explore all creative options. Peter will, unavoidably, take over some aspects of the organization. With the greatest of intentions, some people may be resentful of this. Not only will technology be pushed to its limits.

After a couple of hours chasing lambs around the paddock, we decide to take a break and think about it. Another one. Aside from the fact that it's good to meet old acquaintances again, we're not getting anywhere.

As soon as Peter and his manager leave, followed by Steve, Tony, Mike, and I exhale and jokingly ask, "What the fuck was that all about?" We chuckle about the five of us being unable to do the one thing we all came to Glasgow to do: leave the room with a yes or no. So, with the benefit of the familiar, open, relaxed three-way setting we'd created over the previous twenty years as a trio, we see the obvious and quietly put The Lamb to bed.

In fact, we're so calm that Tony, Mike, and I quickly decide that since we're all here, why don't we do something together?

I settle in at the Peninsula New York Hotel and begin working on this new, third Disney project in earnest in early 2006. I have to, because Tarzan's premiere at the Richard Rodgers Theatre has been pushed back a few months. Being commissioned to write Tarzan on Broadway is a natural extension of writing the soundtrack for the Tarzan film. However, it entails a tremendous level of responsibility, far exceeding that of the film. It also has great potential. I'm hoping that this type of work will enable me to improve my life and be at home with my children. If that's the case, the "Phil Collins" character's retirement can proceed as planned. Maybe I can save my third marriage.

Working on a stage musical improves my creative abilities significantly. I've progressed from creating pop songs to writing material for a whole stage show with an incredible number of moving components.

I spend every day in the Richard Rodgers Theatre. Rehearsing. Listening to the orchestra play my music. Critique, take notes, and attend recording sessions for the cast album. They all believe I'm crazy to be this deep and dedicated.

What I should do is get on a plane, come to Switzerland, and tell Orianne face to face what I tried to convey over the phone: "What are we doing?" I do not want to be without you. I adore my children. I want this to work. What does it take? Is it okay if I disappear for six months while you strive to regain your confidence? "No problem."

But I never do. I just feel like, that's it. There is no rationality, only resignation. I am a stupid bugger.

Still, the Disney juggernaut will not be stopped. Tarzan previews began March 24th, following three months of practice. New York's cultural elite attends them. As a desperate distraction from real life, I attend every preview of "my" show. At one, Tom Schumacher introduces me to Dana Tyler. She is a frequent theatergoer and a news anchor for WCBS-TV's 6 p.m. broadcast. She also hosts a Broadway show for CBS, and the next day she interviews me for a feature.

Dana and I get along really well during the lengthy, in-depth interview. Slowly, slowly, she and I begin to see one other. She's a lovely woman, bright-eyed and intellectual, who has grown up in a very different environment. We communicate emotionally and naturally. She helps me rebuild my self-esteem.

In November 2006, six months after Tarzan's release, I fly to London to join Mike and Tony for the press conference announcing the European leg of the Turn It On Again tour in the summer of 2007.

The situation is gradually improving. I have a Broadway musical, and Phil and Philip Collins are emerging from their slumps, professionally

and personally. Without a question, I miss Orianne and ache for the boys, but I'm trying to go on. She made it clear I had to.

Genesis rehearses in New York before traveling to Geneva. It's enjoyable, but not without drawbacks. We're a weird group because we can never manage to recall how the song goes. It's a nice, straightforward "school band" vibe. Fortunately, our long-time guitarist Daryl Stuermer is typically there to assist us with our sixth-form flailing while we search for the correct sounds and words. A rusty Genesis sounded oddly unsophisticated when we first started rehearsing for anything, but now, a decade, a slew of projects, and two and a half divorces later, I'm having trouble remembering parts from songs written in the 1970s. A lot of words and another life, it appears. However, seeing these old friends again serves as a terrific reminder of why it was so much fun all those years.

I attend these practices to do what I need to do: learn the words and improve my vocals. Meanwhile, Tony and Mike are working on the stage presentation—the lighting design is being done by brilliant production artist and longtime colleague Patrick Woodroffe, and the sets are being designed by acclaimed stage designer Mark Fisher. But I'm not engaged or distracted by that side of things, much to Tony Banks' sometimes evident frustration.

While this was always my view on Genesis, I'll concede there's an underlying message to my semi-detachment. Yes, this is a reunion tour, but not a full-fledged comeback. I believe everyone else involved hoped that in the eighteen months between our Glasgow summit and the commencement of the tour, a new album would have been completed. But that is not something I've been willing to even consider. I absolutely do not want that. With the debut of a Broadway musical and the dissolution of a marriage, I've had enough.

Fundamentally, we don't need to create an album to turn it back on. That would be a backward step. I will not be rejoining Genesis. I'm saying goodbye. Hello, we really should be leaving.

In March 2007, the three of us gather in New York for another news appearance. This one announces the North American portion of the tour, which will begin in Toronto in September. It's six weeks (or "month" in Tony Smith's world) of venues named "Field," "Arena," "Stadium," or "Garden." Agent Giddings and manager Smith have long ignored our call to keep things simple and perform in theaters. The turnout is amazing from the start, and the audience response is fantastic. Europe's stadiums are packed with young people who were not even born when I took over the singing, and they're all very into it. The rain that seems to accompany us over the continent that month doesn't damper their spirits.

It's my first time seeing a few places, most notably Katowice, Poland. There, the weather is biblical—and dangerously so. The thunder and lightning knock the lighting people down from their towers. We're wet onstage during soundcheck, but there are 40,000 Polish fans outside waiting to get in. We cannot let them down. We play through the downpour and end with "The Carpet Crawlers," which has the entire drenched audience singing along with the soaked band. It's emotional, and Dana is in the audience to witness Philip's old band and admirers at their peak.

All these years later, we had a unique addition to our band rider that night: wheelchair ramps. My mother, the only other person who calls me Philip, is present. She is ninety-four, her vision is fading, and she needs to be wheeled into the stadium. But she is there, as devoted to her youngest child's band as she has always been. This is the final time Mum will see me perform. Two years later, she experiences a stroke and is never the same again. She tries to recover, but after additional strokes, she gradually shuts down. June Winifred Collins died on her birthday, November 6, 2011. She is ninety-eight.

I greatly like the entire European run. I have no reservations about returning as frontman; the voice holds up, I'm back in sync with the Genesis material, I relish being a member of a band again, and we all get along brilliantly, as if we've never left. Exactly how friends should be.

Orianne joins the lads for two gigs in Paris and Hannover. Nic and Matt are too young to remember the First Final Farewell Tour, and they want to witness what Dad does firsthand. After the show, Orianne and I got along well, sharing a drink and enjoying the children's excitement. Although we acknowledge that things have changed, it is comforting to know that we are still connected.

And then to Rome for a suitable climax. It's unique to feel like you're playing on old territory. This is Circus Maximus, where performers lived in fear of the imperial thumbs-down millennia ago. I've prepared all of my Italian patter as a precaution. But once I'm out there in front of a half-million people, I realize that all of the fans in the first row are from Brazil, England, Germany, or anywhere other than Italy. But we eventually get a thumbs up, and these aged gladiators live to fight another day.

During the encore of "The Carpet Crawlers," with the audience as witnesses, I tell Tony Banks and Mike Rutherford that I adore them. These men know me better than anyone else in the world, and they get what I'm saying: this is it, no more. The end of the road. No more Genesis for me.

To be honest, instead of another major North American tour, I would have wanted to play Australia, South America, and the Far East. But my limited time is up. Finally, I've realized that my personal life is more important to me than anything else. A month and a half apart from my small boys has been enough to lock the door and toss away the key.

My resolve remains unshaken, even after hearing some terrible news in the middle of the European leg: Tarzan will close in just fifteen months. Ticket sales have been strong, but not enough to support a costly play in the very competitive Broadway market. Obviously, I am devastated by this news, especially since I cannot properly say goodbye to my kid. I'm trapped on tour somewhere, while the entire cast is in tears backstage in New York.

Ironically—and bitterly—it closes on July 8, 2007, the same night Genesis plays at Twickenham. A night with two halves.

But right up until the finish, I am pressured to reconsider calling a halt. Genesis has not "maximized" its managerial opportunities. My indignation over this is reflected in the reunion tour documentary When in Rome. John Giddings and Tony Smith can't help but try to complete their tasks. But if agents, managers, and promoters had anything to do with it, I'd still be out there today. So, if I don't stand firm, I know what will happen. It would turn into an album after three, four, or five months. It's why the documentary cameras capture me firmly standing my ground: "Don't fuck with me, John."

My name is Philip Collins, and I won't be fucked. Not by others, anyway. Unfortunately, my body has different ideas.

During the tour, I developed an issue with my left arm. It reaches a point where I can hardly grip the sticks for "Los Endos," the final song in the set on which I play drums. I attempt heavier sticks and larger cymbals. During the American leg, I visit a variety of medical professionals. I even visit a religion healer. In Montreal, our long-time promoter Donald K. Donald recommends seeing a massage therapist who assisted him after back surgery. I'll do everything to relieve the numbness in my fingers and regain strength in my hands.

I have surgery at the Clinique de Genolier. The surgeons cut open my neck below my left ear, rummage around for the collapsing vertebrae, and screw them together with synthetic calcium.

I recuperate for a year. But even after a year, the fingers on my left hand remain numb. I can't even hold a bread knife—let alone a drumstick. As a left-hander, I rapidly realize how much I rely on my strong hand. I return to my local doctor, based at the Clinique, Dr. Sylviane L'Oizeau, a delightful lady who would go on to aid me greatly in a variety of life-affirming—and even lifesaving—ways. She sends me to Lausanne to see another specialist. Surprise! A new diagnosis. The problem isn't in my neck; it's on the inside of my left elbow, where a nerve is misdirected. It has been squeezed out of position, therefore I will have two operations in early 2008 while the surgeon attempts to re-lay the nerve. This time, the inside of my arm is sliced open, then my left palm.

More recovery. This is the longest I've gone without playing drums since I was twelve. I understand you need to go back on the horse, but I'm not sure the horse is happy about the prospect.

The years 2008 and 2009 are both the best and worst. I've purchased a new home in Féchy, a village just fifteen minutes from our previous family home in Begnins. It's a cozy, modest house that meets all of my needs since I'm on my own. Dana spends much of her time in New York due to nightly business commitments. She makes visits whenever she can, but they are few and far between.

I see a lot of Nic and Matt, and my interactions with Orianne are pleasant. Even though my days as a husband are finished, my days as a hands-on father have only recently begun.

On the negative, recovery from the neck, arm, and hand surgeries is taking much longer than I or any of the medical specialists anticipated. If I had any concerns about the appropriateness of closing up business professionally, my body is making its feelings known. It is waving a white flag.

I put my feet up.

Another red flag appears. Tony Smith wants to know how I am. He is my manager, but he is also a friend. He wants to make sure I don't come to a total standstill in Switzerland. I believe he was put on high alert when I announced that I was relocating there. Even though he knew I was very happy with Orianne, he feared that Europe's most neutral country would kill my creativity to death. He wasn't entirely wrong, and to make matters worse, I'm now alone. But I'm not about to move. Guys are here, so I am here.

"What are you doing?" Tony will speak on the phone.

"I am doing nothing. I'm lying on the sofa, watching cricket."

I feel like I deserve it, especially because my body is clearly in need of rest. I'll take it laying down.

So Tony plays the joker. "Why don't you do a covers album?"

As my astute manager knows, this is something I've always wanted to do. The music of my youth, the stuff that started me on this journey fifty years ago, still thrills and rushes through me. So I propose something along these lines: my interpretations of, and tributes to, the 1960s songs that introduced me to soul and R&B, and that I enjoyed when The Action sprinkled their set with dynamic, Mod-leaning versions. If this is going to be my swan song as a recording artist—which I believe it will be—what better way to end than back where it all began? I'm revisiting my musical roots as my career comes to an end. I'll call this album Going Back to emphasize the concept while also paying homage to the excellent Carole King and Gerry Goffin song "Goin' Back," which is a classic on my hit list.

Yes, it's nostalgia, a chance to do what I wanted to do with my school band, but this time correctly. And nostalgia makes me incredibly alive. It doesn't take long for me to realize that's an extremely lofty order. Even if my drumming and athletic abilities were completely up to par—which they clearly aren't—I'd need some proper musicians to assist me honor those amazing original recordings. Amazingly and thrillingly, Bob Babbitt, Eddie Willis, and Ray Monette—three of The Funk Brothers, who played on so many of the Motown 45s I had collected in my teens—agree to join me.

The irony is that I can't even grip a stick in my left hand while drumming. That is how weak I am. So I taped a stick to my hand. Obviously, that is not ideal. Fortunately, aside from each guy's characteristic fills, the sections are rather simple, which contributes to their timeless appeal.

Working steadily throughout 2009, we eventually recorded twenty-nine tunes. With the album nearly finished by early 2010, I'll be returning to Genesis in March. Just when I thought I was out, they bring me back.

The band is being inducted into the Rock & Roll Hall of Fame in New York. Mike, Tony, Steve, and I all fly in, but Peter is not present; he is in the United Kingdom for tour rehearsals. We're not objecting too much when I claim that his absence very affects none of us. We've long accepted the fact that his schedule is what it is.

Also, he did me a favor. With Peter unavoidably detained elsewhere, any hope of the "re-formed" Genesis performing during the wedding is dead. As my recovery progresses slowly, drumming in public with a stick taped to my hand is clearly not a good appearance.

Three months later, I'm back in New York to accept another honor: the annual Johnny Mercer Award at the 2010 Songwriters Hall of Fame banquet. I'm ecstatic, especially since songwriting is a skill I only recently learned. I'm also surprised: I'm not joking when I tell the BBC on the red carpet that when I got the call asking my appearance, I assumed they wanted me to deliver the award rather than accept it. I'm still not sure whether I'm worthy, and there aren't many groups that would want to have me as a member, but I'll gladly join the songwriters' guild.

These two validations come just in time, since I'll be in Philadelphia a few days after the Songwriters Hall of Fame event to begin a run of gigs in support of the upcoming Going Back. It's a brief run with only seven shows (Philadelphia, New York, London, and the Montreux Jazz Festival), but it's still too long. These shows should be fantastic, but my mind is not where it should be. To make matters worse, once I'm on stage, I can't seem to remember all of the lyrics to the music I grew up with.

I try not to let that event influence my pleasure of the album. Going Back is a personal, intimate, and candid depiction of the 59-year-old artist as a young man. The cover art says it all: a snapshot of me, aged twelve or thirteen, dressed in a beautiful shirt and tie, sitting in our front room at 453 Hanworth Road, behind my Stratford drum kit.

Going Back is released two months after the shows, in September 2010. My eighth solo album debuted at number one in the United Kingdom, becoming my first chart-topping album of new material since Both Sides seventeen years ago. Collins is back! He doesn't truly want to be "back."

Unfortunately, the other universe I believed I could be a part of isn't showing me much love. The Tarzan musical has not resulted in a frenzy of fresh theatrical commissions.

All things considered, by the end of 2010, I'm beginning to believe that this dog has finally had his day. My theatrical career has come to an end with the lackluster Going Back performances. But I can live with it. Just almost.

I decide to give performance one more shot. My left arm and hand are still not totally match-fit, but I tentatively return to the ring. I'm asked to play alongside Eric at a Prince's Trust gala concert in London on November 17, 2010. I am not sure I am ready. However, my relationship with Eric and The Prince's Trust dates back a long time. I can't say no.

But as soon as I sit down to play with the kit, I realize it's a mistake. We're only performing one song together, "Crossroads," but that's one too many. I have no feeling. I think, "I'll never drum again."

So that's it. I have left my band. Drumming has abandoned me. My sparkling Broadway future isn't looking as bright. My marriage has failed for the third time. My girlfriend is stuck in New York. My life is empty.

What shall I fill it with?

I understand. I will have a drink.

Chapter 18: Not Dead Yet

It is the morning following the previous night's hangover. My lost weekend turned into a lost several years, and I almost lost my life. Now I have to engage in some sober introspection and wonder how I ended up there, alone and drowning at the bottom of a bottle.

As 2013 ends and 2014 begins, I am afforded the opportunity to reflect on much of the above. Tony Smith contacts me, Tony Banks, Mike Rutherford, Peter Gabriel, and Steve Hackett. The BBC wants to do a documentary about Genesis' whole career, including all the music we've produced. To a man, we are satisfied. This is the BBC for all the films about the band that have been created throughout the years. The corporation bestows permission and authority, a stamp of quality that is recognized worldwide.

This will be a wonderful time to reflect on everything we've accomplished, both together and apart, and reconnect with one another—and with ourselves. Given my recent brush with mortality, this may be more relevant to me than the other guys. I suggest director John Edginton try something new. Why doesn't he interview all five of us in one room?

Maybe Tony, Mike, Peter, and Steve experience similar sentiments because the proposal was rapidly agreed upon and implemented.

In March 2014, the five of us sat in a large white room in a photographer's studio in Notting Hill, west London. It's the first time we've met since our disastrous Glasgow summit in 2005, and it's also the first time we've been filmed conversing. It's been over forty years since I and my fellow new boy Steve entered, and thirty-five years since Peter left, so there's some catching up to be done. Again, it's strange how we all resort to stereotypes—Steve as the gloomy one, me as the comedian, etc.

With no decisions to make and no duties to fulfill, the attitude in the studio is easygoing and joyful. Each of us seizes the moment to offer our share. Peter once remarks, "When we got it right, we had something which none of us could do on our own."

For my part, I tell Peter something I've never had the opportunity to say explicitly before: "A lot of people have always assumed that I tried to push you out so I could become the singer." I just wanted you to know it wasn't.

I don't think Peter ever believed I was plotting with Machiavellian glee. But, with the cameras rolling, this appears to be a perfect occasion to clear up forty years of rumors and speculation about my "taking over" Genesis. Surprisingly, this confession does not reach the final cut.

The candor extends both ways. In his individual interview in the documentary, Tony comments on my solo success: "It was great for [Phil]." He was our friend, and we wished him well. But you didn't expect him to perform so well at first," he replies, partly kidding. "But it never really went away." He was everywhere for nearly 15 years. You could not get away from him. "Nightmare," he shrugs and smiles. Just as importantly, he adds that Genesis was unique in that we were able to operate the band and our individual careers in such close proximity for so long. Hence the documentary's title—Genesis: Together and Apart.

During a lunch break during filming, Tony Smith, Dana, Steve's wife Jo, and the band discuss what's new in their life, how everyone's kids are growing up, and what they're doing. I am reminded how wonderful it is to have friends like this.

There has been talk for a while about a new compilation CD, and its premise embodies the lifetime, all-for-one conviviality of this gathering. For the first time ever, the greatest of the band is combined with the best of the five separate careers. This three-CD, 37-track, nearly four-hour career-spanning box set is chronologically ordered and stoutly democratic, with three tracks from each of us. I mostly stay out of discussions about which Genesis tracks will appear—I trust the other guys to carry that torch—but from my albums, I choose "In the Air Tonight" (it would be rude not to), "Easy Lover" (partly because it is not on any of my studio albums), and "Wake Up Call" from Testify (because it is my favorite song on an underappreciated album).

When it comes to naming and dressing this box, it's astonishing how simple it is. Although there is some corner-cutting, we've all matured gracefully, and the process is mostly diva-free. The Big Tree and Its Splinters is a possibility, but we eventually settle on Peter's notion, R-Kive, with the spelling hinting at "today."

R-Kive is launched in September, and the five of us attend the documentary's premiere in London's Haymarket on October 4, 2014, just before it airs on the BBC. It's a beautiful, relaxing evening spent with many old friends, including Hugh Padgham and Richard MacPhail, among others. At the screening, everyone laughs in the appropriate places, and no one leaves in a huff.

Right now, I'm also considering my legacy in other areas. Sixty years after first seeing the Disney Davy Crockett film, and nearly two decades after Orianne's first gift of an Alamo artifact to me, I have accumulated a sizable collection of battle-related antiquities and militaria. I even wrote a book, The Alamo and Beyond: A Collector's Journey (2012), at the request of a Texas publishing business. By some estimates, mine is the world's largest private collection, worth around $10 million.

While monetary value means little to me, historical value is extremely important. Now, following my inebriated dance-with-death, I'm more concerned than ever about what will happen to my collection after I die.

So, to avoid any unpleasant arguing over who gets my rare Crockett musket, and just in case a sibling conflict breaks out over my prized Mexican cannonballs, I decide to donate my 200-piece collection to a suitable museum or institution in San Antonio.

After consulting with friends and experts in Texas, I've decided that the best method is to return this collection to its rightful owner: the Alamo, located in downtown San Antonio and the Lone Star State's most popular tourist attraction.

On June 26, 2014, we made a public declaration outside the Alamo, and I returned in October to watch the collection arrive from Switzerland. It will be housed in a museum, as part of a $100 million renovation of the Alamo complex. On the floor of the Texas House of Representatives, I am also designated as an Honorary Texan. The little Hounslow child inside me still can't believe it. If you hear me speaking with a Texas twang, feel free to clip me around the ear.

Meanwhile, back at my former day job, all of this activity—not to mention the public demonstrations of camaraderie between my former bandmates and me—has sparked another round of speculation about a Genesis reunion. As ever, I'm not sure people have fully considered this—if the five of us did return on the road after a forty-year hiatus, it would have to be the Peter-era band. This would entail performing the material we created when the five of us were together, and the truth is that that material has a more limited audience. Concertgoers will receive "Can-Utility and the Coastliners," "Fountain of Salmacis," but not "I Can't Dance" or "Invisible Touch."

All that said, there's a more pressing, more practical issue: I'm still not up to the job of drumming. Furthermore, I am not really interested in performing.

I know this because, in September 2014, just before the release of R-Kive, at Tony Smith's gentle but forceful urging, I gathered a small group of core musicians in Miami. I'll be there anyhow to see the boys, so I don't view it as a big deal or commitment. This will be more of a pleasant thrash about rather than a rehearsal. It's also a sop to Nic and Matt, who are eager to watch the old man perform live. So I agree to a carefree three-week rehearsal-room frolic through the old material.

To add some youthful energy, I recruited Jason Bonham to play drums, and we began working through some songs. It all sounds wonderful at first, with Jason busting some major butt during the hard numbers, but I quickly become distracted. I'm wondering: "Do I really need to sing 'Against All Odds' again, now?"

I'm embarrassed to admit that I'm starting to act like a sixty-three-year-old schoolboy. I go to bed early, take a sick day the next day, and then skip work entirely. I put keyboardist Brad Cole in control of the band, and they perform without me. I'm completely uninterested.

Unfortunately, this flakiness raises alarms worldwide. Tony learns about it in London, and Dana hears about it in New York. They understandably fear the worse. Before I know it, Dana has stormed into my Miami hotel room, demanding explanations. Why do I skip rehearsals? Am I drinking again?

I'm polite—"No, honestly, I'm not drinking"—but also upset. Tony had alerted her, so she took the day off work, flew from New York, managed to get a key to my room, and burst in, ready for confrontation and intervention. Of course, she has my best interests at heart, and she has been through a nightmare with me in recent years. However, I do not appreciate being treated as a child.

By this stage, our relationship had deteriorated slightly. I've been spending more and more time in Miami to be with the boys, and I believe she has a nagging suspicion that Orianne and I are getting closer again. This surely doesn't help matters.

We're both upset, and that leads to openness. Dana expects to be married by now, but I have no intention of walking down the aisle for the fourth time. Important things are stated, and some tears are shed. She stays overnight in my hotel room, albeit at arm's length, and when I wake up in the morning, she is gone. After eight years, our partnership has ended.

If my behavior, both personally and professionally, exhibits all of the characteristics of semi-detachment, it is possible that other attachments are throwing me off balance, in a positive way. Dana's suspicions are not unjustified. Orianne and I are approaching again.

Since she and the boys moved to Miami in July 2012, I've flown there every other week, staying at the Ritz Carlton on South Beach. Some of the initial meeting was undoubtedly influenced by alcohol. However, since I've been dry, the relationships and intimacy have gradually improved. At the same time, Orianne's marriage was collapsing. We frequently tell each other that we should never have divorced, that we miss each other, and that we miss having a family.

Orianne returns to Switzerland in late December 2014 for spinal surgery to free blocked nerves. Unfortunately, she experiences spasms while under the knife. As a result, Orianne is completely paralyzed on her right side. She will not be leaving her bed, let alone Switzerland, anytime soon. When she calls to tell me, I believe she is joking.

After spending New Year's with the boys in New York as planned, I return them to Miami. Following several chats with her husband, we agree that I should go see Orianne first. When I arrive in Switzerland, my ex-wife greets me in a wheelchair, a haunting shell of her former self. We are both devastated.

I stay for a week before flying home to be both mum and dad to the boys. Orianne is trapped in rehab in Switzerland until early March 2015, when she finally flies home. She, the kids, and I are all relieved and pleased.

However, this has been a period of healing all around. We've been open and honest with each other in recent months, expressing our actual thoughts and feelings. We have decided that Orianne and I will reconcile, if not un-divorce. When we tell Nicholas and Mathew, they are overjoyed. In fact, Matt adds something amazing: "You know, I had a wish on my tenth birthday that this would happen." The concept that the kids wanted this to happen is really heartwarming.

Together, we begin looking at houses in Miami. My criteria include a location where Matt can have a little football pitch and Nic can have a small studio to rehearse with his band and hone his drumming talents. We find the ideal location, which turns out to be Jennifer Lopez's old home (I only learn out later when Joely informs me). I sign the paperwork in June 2015, and we settle into a family home on Miami Beach. Now we are four again. Actually, now we are five. Orianne's second marriage produced a son, Andrea, who spends a lot of time with us. Complicated? With my background, nothing is too complicated.

It takes until early 2016 for word to spread that I am back with my third ex-wife. The giddier areas of the international press were filled with shock and snark.

Whatever, I'm back with my ex-wife and boys, and we're all quite happy.

The Collins family is a funny bunch. I know how it appears: a shattered, dispersed family ruled over—in the loosest sense of the term—by Phil, who has three wives. But, despite everything, we laugh about it. Love will find a way.

I carry guilt for each of my children. Honestly, I feel guilty about everything. All the times I was away, all the moments I missed, all the occasions when a tour or an album interfered with a nice home life, or house renovations. Music made and unmade me.

It will not do this again. Now I'm back to being Nic and Matt's father, and I'm grateful every time I'm present for a football game, a school band rehearsal, or some schoolwork.

However, happiness breeds guilt: the happier I am with Nic and Matt, the more guilty I feel for not being present for the older ones. I wasn't there to share those same chats or experience the same domestic bliss as Joely, Simon, and Lily.

We're a work in progress—name a family that isn't—but I think we're doing fairly well, considering. Joely began acting, won numerous prizes, and is now a producer working in television and internet. She lives in Vancouver with her Dutch husband, Stefan, and their beautiful daughter, Zoe. Born on October 26, 2009, she made me a grandfather at the tender age of fifty-eight. They are delightfully joyful and serve as an example to all.

Respect to Simon: he made things difficult for himself by attempting to follow the old man's line of work. He's faced some difficulties, both emotionally and professionally, but he's fought hard to overcome them. He's an excellent drummer, and as a vocalist, he's discovered his voice. He's received numerous awards in the progressive rock genre, and he's done an excellent job of establishing a fan base and finding an audience. Making albums, especially on your own terms, is a tremendous accomplishment in today's music market. He's a headstrong musician who knows what he wants. God knows where he got that from.

Simon and I finally played drums together in 2008 on his album U Catastrophe. He wrote "The Big Bang," a song for both of us to play, and I flew to Las Vegas to record with him. It's a really quick tune, loosely based on the Genesis drum duets, and he really pushed me through my paces. I just barely made it. It's a terrific track, and I believe that working with my oldest son was, unknowingly, my final hurrah as a drummer. Which seems fitting.

Lily is another source of pride for her parents. A youthful modeling stint led to a successful acting career. She is currently filming the lead role in Amazon's upcoming drama series based on F. Scott Fitzgerald's The Last Tycoon. She's been in a few high-profile Hollywood films, including The Blind Side (with Sandra Bullock) and Mirror Mirror (with Julia Roberts), in which she plays Snow White, and she stars alongside Warren Beatty in his new picture Rules Don't Apply. She is socially concerned and engaged, and an excellent public speaker. She is also participating in an anti-bullying project in Los Angeles.

Brother Clive continues to make a living by painting cartoons and has received numerous international awards. He received the MBE in 2011. I am so proud of him.

Sister Carole is as happy as she has ever been. She has been married to Bob 42 years. Following her long career as a professional ice skater, she took over Mum's position as a theatrical agent. She played a nosy neighbor in Buster, and she did an excellent job.

Unfortunately, my darling mother could not join us tonight. After suffering her first stroke in April 2009, she steadily declined until her death on November 6, 2011, just two years shy of turning 100.

I was able to spend some time with her before it ended. I'd come in from Switzerland to see her at Barbara Speake's house in Ealing, sit by the bed, stroke her head as she fell asleep, and thought, "If only I could have done this with my dad."

The one positive aspect is that Mum's illness brought Carole, Clive, and I closer together. Because of our geographical distance, we had grown accustomed to not conversing for extended periods of time. We spent a lot of time discussing and visiting Mum in the hospital while she was sick.

My mother appreciated my profession and believed she had done well by assisting and encouraging me. But it's still difficult for me to accept the idea that Dad died before seeing any of my accomplishments. Where is he, and what are his thoughts on the situation? Hope he has forgiven me for avoiding the London Assurance office job. I hope I made dad proud.

I am undeniably fortunate. I had a long career, and I think the music has aged well. For one, particular moments in my back collection are linked to specific locations and times. If a TV show or film wants to convey the high 1980s with immediate auditory shorthand, "In the Air Tonight" appears to be the best option. On the other hand, it's fantastic to hear younger artists identifying as admirers. My acceptance ratings among the hip-hop community are quite strong. It's a tremendous delight to have my songs covered by Lil' Kim, Brandy, and Bone Thugs-N-Harmony; Kanye West spoke to me as an inspiration, and there was an entire album, Urban Renewal (2001), of hip-hop and R&B versions. This makes me extremely pleased.

There appears to have been much more of an increase recently. Pharrell Williams was invited to remix Face Value. His response was, "Why do you want to do that?" "I like it as is." Lorde and Ryan Tedder, composer extraordinaire and OneRepublic frontman, are also big fans. And then there's Adele.

I missed her rise because I was so deep in my Drinking Years. Actually, I had not heard of her. However, when she called me in October 2013 to collaborate on her third album, I was delighted to meet. I did a lot of homework and was very impressed. She's a great talent, one of the most significant of our time.

This November, she pays me a visit at the Dorchester Hotel in London. She phones from the lobby, and I tell her about the room. She arrives with a security guard. Once he has confirmed that she is safe with me, she instructs him to wait below.

And there we are: just me and Adele. She's precisely what you'd expect: a nice, if not sweary, north London girl whose down-to-earth nature is unaffected by her status as the pre-eminent musician of the day and all-conquering savior of the music industry.

I make her a cup of tea and try to mask my anxieties. I feel as if I'm being auditioned, but that's my insecurities. Adele could be thinking, "Blimey, Phil Collins is fahkin' older than I thought!" Some people associate my image with a specific pop video from a particular year. Let us hope it isn't "You Can't Hurry Love."

She takes out a USB stick, connects it into my laptop, and plays some music, citing a Fleetwood Mac vibe. It's great. And it is quite long. I don't know how to reply or what is being requested of me, so I say, "I'd need to hear it again."

Adele replies, "I'll send it to you, and you can finish it."

I learn the piece on my piano in New York and then add some bits in my small studio down the street in Manhattan. After a while, I sent another email: "Are you waiting for me, or am I waiting for you?"

Adele apologizes and explains that she is relocating, changing email addresses, caring for the baby, and other responsibilities.

I subsequently read her saying that it was still too early in the writing and recording process for the album that would become the smash hit 25, that she wasn't ready, and that she still thinks I'm amazing. That is cool. It was a beautiful little interlude that boosted my self-esteem.

Unfortunately, before I can start swaggering about town calling myself Adele's new best friend, I need to deal with some more medical difficulties.

In October 2015, I wake up in Miami with a severe pain down my right side and limp in to visit the wonderful, not to mention famed, Dr. Barth Green. You could call him the Adele of the spinal surgery world.

His considered medical opinion is that, to put it mildly, my back "is totally shot." But don't worry; Dr. Green has the technology and can recreate me. He takes me into the operating room, inserts eight screws into my spine, and promises me that everything will be OK.

I hobble home to rest, where I soon fall in the bedroom and fracture my right foot. Back to hospital, back to surgery. During physical rehabilitation, I had another fall and refracture my foot.

"Interestingly," during these foot-related traumas, I discover that the "sprain" I sustained after landing heavily at the end of "Domino" on the 1986 Genesis tour of Australia had actually broken off a bit of bone. Also, "interestingly," I've learned that all those vocal cord-easing cortisone injections may have conspired to make my bones brittle. I could chuckle if I weren't in so much pain.

All things considered, it appears that chunks are dropping off of me. Am I paying for all those years of drumming? It began at age five and has now lasted sixty years.

After leaving the hospital and recovering, I am eventually compelled to pick up a stick. Unfortunately, it is a walking stick.

Ironically, this period coincides with my being compelled to present myself to the foreign press. I need to start the long-term promotion for the 2016 reissues of my solo albums. The year-long ad is called "Take a Look at Me Now," and it comes at a time when I'd like people not look at me, this limping, hobbling semi-invalid.

Even so, these media encounters have lifted my spirits. For the first time in what feels like an eternity, the interviews and the ensuing published stories have received glowing reviews. It's all a little giddy.

So, whether it was owing to my zeal, the writer's enthusiasm, or a mix of the two, a news piece appeared in Rolling Stone. "Phil Collins Plotting Comeback," reads the headline. "I Am No Longer Retired."

The magazine quotes me as saying, "I got very involved in these reissues..." I am easily flattered. "It would be silly not to make more music if people rediscover the old stuff and show interest." And then: "I don't think I want a long tour. But I want to play stadiums in Australia and the Far East, and this is the only way to do so. But a part of me still wants to work in theaters, so we'll see."

Did I actually say all that? It was probably the drugs talking, but it's an intriguing suggestion. A man with a limp who can barely walk, let alone rock makes this declaration. Rumors of my return may have been overblown, not least by me.

Even BBC Radio 4's very serious current affairs show Today deems my reported retirement to be a newsworthy subject at breakfast time.

A nation chokes on its cornflakes before breaking out its eighties/nineties party clothes.

Printed in Dunstable, United Kingdom

72893644R00100